Praise for *Optimizing Learning: Thinking Skills, Technology, Teaming*

"This joint effort by the accomplished authors compels an educator to explore technology and collaboration in meaningful ways for students and teachers. The text is engaging and promotes numerous practices, essential strategies, and equitable considerations for any new or seasoned teacher committed to ensuring that the imperative objective always occurs—student achievement."

Joyce Nguyen Hernandez
College Access Coordinator/Department of
Equity, Inclusion, and Innovation
Kansas City Public Schools

"With this book, educators can access an updated and powerful resource to help students think more critically, use technology wisely, and engage in effective teaming. Drs. Caulfield, Jennings, and May-Washington have provided an informative tool for teachers to utilize across grade levels that will give them the ability to take a look at their current practices and make adjustments in their classrooms to ensure excellent instruction and lead to excellent learning."

John O'Connor
President of Cristo Rey High School

"I'm convinced that one of the central changes needed in schools is to see youth as people who can and should help improve their community as they learn academic subjects. We must change the paradigm of how adults instruct and students learn.

I've seen software that helps students identify a current problem, (school or society) think about how to solve it, use skills they are developing to help solve it, and then reflect on what went well, what needed to be improved the next time. as described in this Optimizing Learning book."

Dr. Joe Nathan
Director, Center for School

"Timely, well-written, and chock full of teaching tools and tips for meeting the challenges of twenty-first century teaching. Optimizing Learning is the intervention needed for K-12 education in this brave, new world in which we live and learn. Every teacher—from those just starting their careers to those with decades of experience—will benefit from reading this book, and adopting its strategies."

James M. Thomas, PhD
Associate Professor of Sociology
University of Mississippi
Proud alum of Lincoln College, Preparatory
Academy in Kansas City, Missouri

"In a world where students are increasingly isolated through technology, the ideas and concepts presented offer a welcome recourse to the 'closing off' of social/cognitive development.

The work lays out in a detailed manner but with feasible options, how to implement goals and strategies that will have beneficial outcomes for students and teachers. I fully plan on sharing these ideas with my colleagues and implementing the strategies in my own classrooms."

Bill McGee
Social Studies Department Chair/Honor Council Chair
The Pembroke Hill School

Optimizing Learning

Optimizing Learning

Thinking Skills, Technology, Teaming

Joan Caulfield, Wayne Jennings, and Siabhan May-Washington

ROWMAN & LITTLEFIELD
Lanham • Boulder • New York • London

Published by Rowman & Littlefield
An imprint of The Rowman & Littlefield Publishing Group, Inc.
4501 Forbes Boulevard, Suite 200, Lanham, Maryland 20706
www.rowman.com

86-90 Paul Street, London EC2A 4NE

Copyright © 2021 by Joan Caulfield, Wayne Jennings, and Siabhan May-Washington

All rights reserved. No part of this book may be reproduced in any form or by any electronic or mechanical means, including information storage and retrieval systems, without written permission from the publisher, except by a reviewer who may quote passages in a review.

British Library Cataloguing in Publication Information Available

Library of Congress Cataloging-in-Publication Data

Names: Caulfield, Joan, 1940- author. | Jennings, Wayne, 1930- author. | May-Washington, Siabhan, 1966- author.
Title: Optimized learning : thinking skills, technology, teaming / Joan Caulfield, Wayne Jennings, and Siabhan May-Washington.
Description: Lanham, Maryland : Rowman & Littlefield Publishers, 2021. | Includes bibliographical references and index. | Summary: "With this book, educators can access an updated and powerful resource to help students think more critically, use technology wisely, and engage in effective teaming. This book lays out in a detailed manner how to implement goals and strategies that will have beneficial outcomes for students and teachers"— Provided by publisher.
Identifiers: LCCN 2021044017 (print) | LCCN 2021044018 (ebook) | ISBN 9781475857047 (cloth) | ISBN 9781475857054 (paperback) | ISBN 9781475857061 (epub)
Subjects: LCSH: Effective teaching. | Educational planning. | Critical thinking—Study and teaching. | Education—Technological innovations.
Classification: LCC LB1025.3 .C396 2021 (print) | LCC LB1025.3 (ebook) | DDC 371.102—dc23
LC record available at https://lccn.loc.gov/2021044017
LC ebook record available at https://lccn.loc.gov/2021044018

Dedication

We dedicate this book in honor of hardworking teachers across the world. Teaching is an exhausting profession that can drain one's energy and requires patience, yet few professions are more rewarding. When teachers have the right tools and strategies, they accomplish amazing feats. This book will provide teachers with additional strength to carry on.

We wish to individually extend our heartfelt appreciation to our loved ones.

I, Joan, am grateful for the support of my husband Dr. Alan Warne and my family.

I, Wayne, am grateful for the many educators who have supported me professionally to pioneer new ways of educating students—and for a supportive family.

I, Siabhan, am forever grateful for the loving sacrifices that my late parents Floyd and Aritta May made to ensure that I received outstanding guidance and education. Finally, I would like to also thank my husband Rick Washington and our children Brandon, Lauren, and Taryn for their unending support, love, humor, and encouragement.

As a writing team, we thank all of the teachers from whom we have learned!

Contents

Foreword by Jeffrey T. Loeb, PhD — xi
Preface — xv
Introduction — xvii

  1 Mastering the Power of Thinking — 1
  2 Leveraging the Power of Technology — 75
  3 Harnessing the Power of Teaming — 93

Epilogue — 111
Bibliography — 113
Index — 115
About the Authors — 117

Foreword

By Jeffrey T. Loeb, PhD

To say the world has shifted over the past two years is an enormous understatement. Educators especially must recognize the vast and most likely permanent shifts the worldwide pandemic has wrought—in our lives and in our classrooms. As just one example, the necessity for distance learning has made technology use almost teleological. The same might be said for independent projects and small-group collaboration. The authors of this book feel that these circumstances have made it crucial to adjust, and even remake, many of the teaching methods advocated in previous editions. By providing solid, classroom grounding for their ideas throughout, they provide the possibility—for newly minted and experienced educators alike—to forge ahead into a new era.

The idea for a follow-up edition on improving the science and craft of teaching arose about two years ago. The writers' discussions about the already-rapid emergence of new resources were just beginning when COVID-19 emerged. They realized right away that two things had changed forever: the "traditional" teacher-centered classroom model had grown even more hoary (if not nearly obsolete) and the use of technology had suddenly moved to the center of all disciplines. At the same time, they recognize that individual achievement is only enhanced by collaboration and the sharing of information. In no way do the authors favor abandoning the tried-and-true—the value of sweat-equity, for instance, or the sudden lightbulb of a breakthrough—but rather insist that adaptation and cooperation are key for those who wish to avoid joining the proverbial hindmost.

Teaching has always already been a challenging and even draining profession, of course. In the impending face of incipient absences and greater unevenness in student progress, though, the authors immediately knew teachers would be taxed with even greater day-to-day decisions. Curriculum guides could provide some direction, of course, but both the details in and depth of such manuals are themselves often overwhelming, especially to those new to the profession. And for anyone faced with a variety of grade levels or disciplines, the challenge of facing day-to-day strategies might begin to seem insurmountable. It is in the presence of such realities that the team of authors has brought forth a new, extended edition that expands on sound, well-worn ground with new immediately employable teaching strategies.

For readers who haven't seen earlier editions, this book is a follow-up to *Bridging the Learning/Assessment Gap-Showcase Teaching*, written by Dr. Joan Caulfield and Dr. Wayne Jennings. For those new to the profession or those unacquainted with the methods of independent learning, especially in the realms of technology and teaming, this edition seems crucial in helping educators to meet looming challenges. The newest collaborator, Dr. Siabhan May-Washington, who has served as both an instructional supervisor and a school administrator, specializes in strategic teaching, collaborative teaming, and technology-assisted learning, augmenting the extensive knowledge of Doctors Caulfield and Jennings in the areas of brain-based research and thinking skills. The joint aim of these writers is to expand on the prior editions with new ideas for teachers to achieve a solid grounding in both the classroom use of technology and the power of teaming. They thus emphasize aligned instruction, optimized thinking skills, and experiential learning, as well as presenting hands-on suggestions for utilizing these powerful concepts through independent learning and computer-based collaboration.

The authors insist throughout that growth is possible for both teachers (of any experience level) and learners—providing for the first an environment of clear goals and cooperation, and for the second, a how-to in becoming leaders themselves, especially with their already-existing capacity for networking and knowledge of digital technology. The first section comprises, delineates, and describes scores of classroom strategies for creating and then harnessing the flow of ideas that pour forth from an open exchange and critique of ideas. The second is a veritable hands-on of already-existing digital programs for all comers, expert and novice alike.

I have to honestly say, as a longtime teacher myself—and one who struggled mightily with the digital chasm that began emerging three decades ago—that there is more than enough here to propel any educator to classroom success for many, many years, and to do so with a sense of the joy and achievement that we all strive for in teaching. The highly adaptable, concrete suggestions presented herein will immediately supply ambitious teachers with the means of transforming the classroom into a proverbial window-on-the-universe, with the students then becoming the explorers of the possible in this brave new world.

Preface

This book is designed to help teachers establish powerful strategies to encourage thinking skills, the use of technologies, and teaming techniques to help students learn. Regardless of grade level or school type, these strategies are important and can help teachers successfully implement their curriculum.

A common trait among all teachers is an ardent desire to prepare their students to reach high levels of performance. The majority of teachers are in the profession because they genuinely love to teach, and they care about their students. Teachers are willing to work tirelessly each and every day to prepare their students for the future.

Our goal in writing *Optimizing Learning* is to give teachers pragmatic support and effective tools to facilitate excellent learning. Many educational books are unfortunately very unwieldy and quite difficult for novice and experienced teachers, alike, to gather straightforward guidance. This book is a practical resource that can help teachers design lessons that will catalyze their students to think critically, use technology wisely, and engage in teaming more effectively.

It is a mistake for teachers to fall into a stagnant rut of not exploring new ideas that can add vivacity to the classroom environment. We have outlined clear methods and advice that can be helpful to any teacher. Students of all abilities benefit from thinking strategies, technology aids, and teaming techniques regardless of their skill levels.

A prepared, intelligent teacher must be adept in applying the most appropriate teaching strategy depending on the learning objectives at hand. It is up to the teacher to implement the proper strategies that best suit their classroom learners' needs.

In addition, teachers must help educate their students' parents about the strategies that they are using in the classroom. Teachers should also be encouraged to consult with, and seek support from, colleagues and instructional coaches, as they attempt to implement the strategies.

The most important thing teachers need to remember is to explore multiple methods of meeting their students' learning needs. As teachers will encounter diverse learners in their classrooms, it is important to have an array of available strategies ready to use. Raising student achievement levels does not happen effortlessly. Classroom teachers must stay the course in developing viable methods that promote thinking, use of technology, and effective teaming.

Without the assiduous efforts of classroom teachers, our students will not be prepared for the future. Teachers play a pivotal role in ensuring that all students improve their thinking skills, use technology effectively, and develop proficiencies in teaming, to meet the challenges of the twenty-first century.

Introduction

This book includes user-friendly, practical information organized in three chapters to address specific teaching and learning issues. Each chapter addresses specific skills and best practices for activating cognition and achievement in the classroom. The book is organized to address thinking skills first, then the benefits of incorporating technology into classroom instruction, followed by fun techniques that allow students to work and team together.

Throughout the book, there are graphic organizers, diagrams, and illustrations to help highlight important sections of each chapter. Each section also includes self-analysis rater scales to allow readers to assess their understanding and/or skills to implement the techniques.

In a very concise format, this book covers essential elements of teaching that will enable teachers to improve how they deliver instruction to their students. We know that teachers are very busy and welcome resources that are clear and comprehensive in scope. We have condensed the most helpful approaches to help both novice and experienced teachers, alike, optimize learning for their students.

Our greatest hope is that not only will teachers use this book for themselves, but that they will also share it with colleagues near and far. We hope that all teachers will find encouragement, assistance, and invaluable tips to serve them for years to come.

Chapter 1

Mastering the Power of Thinking

ESSENTIAL QUESTION: *HOW CAN THINKING SKILLS IMPROVE STUDENT LEARNING? WHAT TO TEACH?*

The answer to this question is weighty—no question about it! Elementary teachers are responsible for teaching the so-called 3 Rs: *r*eading, [w]*r*iting, and '*r*ithmetic. Secondary teachers are relegated to teaching the disciplines of history, literature, mathematics, and the sciences.

This book is made fresh by the addition of strategies not just centered on the 3 Rs, but the 3 Ts: *t*hinking skills, *t*echnology, and the power of *t*eaming. These three strategies are essential for success. All teachers are guided by national and state standards and curriculum committees. This chapter will focus on how teaching skills can improve student learning.

It is trickier to answer *how* to teach. Every teacher begins the school year thinking that it will be the best year ever. After years of experience, research, and classroom observation, it is clear that teachers aspire to be not just good, but great.

Some of the methods that will be shared are not necessarily new, yet they provide teachers with fresh, exciting, and innovative ways to reflect on their classroom teaching. Just think, for example, would Socrates have imagined that his seminar method would still be so highly touted today? Each teacher reading this book may become the teacher that generations will eulogize.

EMPIRICAL SCIENTIFIC THINKING METHOD

The seventeenth-century empirical scientific thinking method involves careful observation and being skeptical about what one observes. This is a valuable method to encourage student thinking. It includes training students to think in a five-step process in which they will:

1. Observe—to pay close attention to something.
2. Question—to ask for more information.
3. Hypothesize—to make an educated guess.
4. Predict—to forecast an outcome.
5. Test the prediction—to perform activities that allow for a trial of the hypothesis.

This method, tried and true, is important today and will work for any discipline (how to throw a free throw in basketball, how to identify good writing traits, or how to design a building). It is essential to give students several models to consider in their thinking. The more modern term for this is metacognitive skills.

Take a moment now to self-assess the value of incorporating the Empirical Scientific Method in your classroom. Place an X for your self-appraisal. On a scale of 1 to 10 rank your use of it. Selecting #10 would mean confidence about applying the method in the classroom; whereas, a #1 indicates low confidence about its appropriateness for your classroom practice.

1   2   3   4   5   6   7   8   9   10

Whom are you teaching? Jokingly, you might say "human beings." When you think about it, aren't they really humans who are becoming, or "human becomings?" In any given class there may be a future Nobel winner, a gifted artist, an Olympic star, or a best-selling author.

No one has the power to change the world more than a teacher, whether he or she is a parent, a coach, a third-grade teacher, or a professor. Typically, teachers are not educated about what thinking means and/or how reflective thinking practices can improve student learning.

Before reading on, reflect on what thinking means to you? As a teacher, if you tell the parents of your students that you are teaching their children thinking skills, how would you define it? The following star graphic will help provide a clearer perspective (figure 1.1).

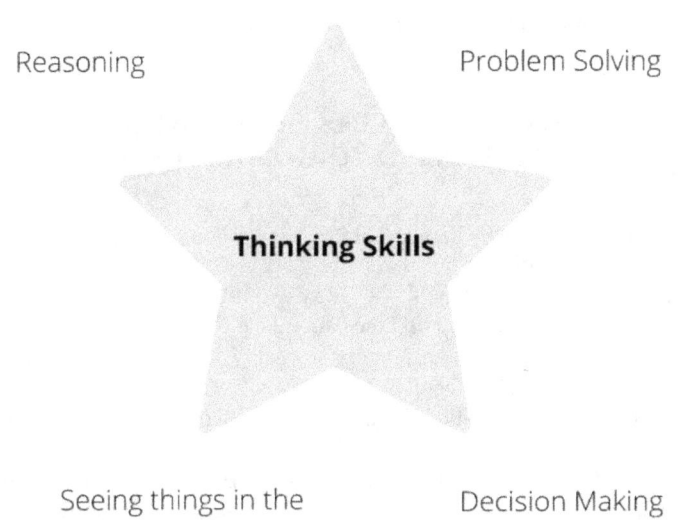

Figure 1.1 **Star Graphic.** *Source:* Wayne Jennings & Joan Caulfield.

TAXONOMY OF EDUCATIONAL OBJECTIVES

In 1956, Benjamin Bloom developed the now-famous Taxonomy of Educational Objectives. The six levels are arranged progressively from the lowest level of thinking, simple recall, to higher orders of thinking that are integrated with previous learning. Guskey theorized that teachers could apply Bloom's levels to help all students learn.[1] Our suggestion is to teach students the six levels of Bloom and to utilize them when you are teaching or designing a test.

The six levels are:

Knowledge
Comprehension
Application
Analysis
Synthesis
Evaluation

Amy Reilly, an elementary school teacher in Lawrence, Kansas, shared an example of how she applied Bloom's Levels of Learning when teaching *Goldilocks and the Three Bears*.

BLOOM'S LEVELS OF LEARNING
(AS APPLIED TO *GOLDILOCKS*)

Evaluation: Judge whether Goldilocks was good or bad. Defend your opinion.
Synthesis: Propose how the story would be different if it were Goldilocks and the Three Fish.
Analysis: Compare this story to reality. What events could not really happen?
Application: Demonstrate what Goldilocks would use if she came to your house.
Comprehension: Explain why Goldilocks liked Baby Bear's chair the best.
Knowledge: List the items used by Goldilocks while she was in the Bear's house.

It is highly effective to give students keywords for each level and to ask them to write two questions for each level.

When teachers use Bloom's Level of Learning, they equip their students with metacognitive skills and the ability to make their thinking visible and reflective.

One way to spice up a classroom is to put the names of the six levels of Bloom on a separate strip of paper. Then, based on the curriculum, let a student draw one out of the box and create a question based on that domain. Another technique is to ask students to make a list of words for each domain. Students experience tremendous satisfaction when they understand their thinking.

Take a moment now to reflect on the value of incorporating Bloom's Levels of Learning in your classroom. Place an X by your level of confidence evaluating its appropriateness for your classroom practice.

1   2   3   4   5   6   7   8   9   10

CATEGORIZING INTELLIGENCES

In 1983, Howard Gardner, a Harvard professor, wrote *Frames of Mind*, and the book continues to influence teaching today. What is significant is that Gardner states that everyone has all kinds of intelligence in different quantities.[2] The key is to help students identify their intelligence and teach them to strengthen their weaker abilities.

Gardner's eight categories that intelligence fall into are:

Linguistic Intelligence ("Word Smart")
Logical Mathematical Intelligence ("Numbers Smart")
Spatial Intelligence ("Picture Smart")
Bodily-Kinesthetic Intelligence ("Body Smart")
Musical Intelligence ("Music Smart")
Interpersonal Intelligence ("People Smart")
Intrapersonal Intelligence ("Self Smart")
Naturalistic Intelligence ("Nature Smart")

Students enjoy learning about musical intelligence. One way to assess their strengths is to use one of the many sites on the internet. For example, view the following helpful site: (http.//literacyworks.org/mi/assessment/findyourstrengths.html).

Teachers need to know their strengths and vary their teaching. It is said teachers tend to teach to their own strength.

Included below are strategies for each intelligence.

The intelligence assessment site, as shown in figure 1.2, can help you determine which intelligences are strongest for you. If you're a teacher or tutor, you can also use it to find out which intelligence your learner uses most often. Many thanks to Dr. Terry Armstrong for graciously allowing us to use his questionnaire.

Instructions: Read each statement carefully. Choose one of the five buttons for each statement indicating how well that statement describes you.

1 = Statement does not describe you at all
2 = Statement describes you very little
3 = Statement describes you somewhat
4 = Statement describes you pretty well
5 = Statement describes you exactly

1.	I pride myself on having a large vocabulary.
2.	Using numbers and numerical symbols is easy for me.
3.	Music is very important to me in daily life.
4.	I always know where I am in relation to my home
5.	I consider myself an athlete.
6.	I feel like people of all ages like me.
7.	I often look for weaknesses in myself that I see in others.
8.	The world of plants and animals is important to me.
9.	I enjoy learning new words and do so easily.
10.	I often develop equations to describe relationships and/or to explain my observations.
11.	I have wide and varied musical interests including both classical and contemporary.
12.	I do not get lost easily and can orient myself with either maps or landmarks.
13.	I feel really good about being physically fit.
14.	I like to be with all different types of people.
15.	I often think about the influence I have on others.
16.	I enjoy my pets.
17.	I love to read and do so daily.
18.	I often see mathematical ratios in the world around me.
19.	I have a very good sense of pitch, tempo, and rhythm.
20.	Knowing directions is easy for me.
21.	I have good balance and eye-hand coordination and enjoy sports which use a ball.
22.	I respond to all people enthusiastically, free of bias or prejudice.
23.	I believe that I am responsible for my actions and who I am.
24.	I like learning about nature.
25.	I enjoy hearing challenging lectures.
26.	Math has always been one of my favorite classes.
27.	My music education began when I was younger and continues today.
28.	I have the ability to represent what I see by drawing or painting.
29.	My outstanding coordination and balance let me excel in high-speed activities.
30.	I enjoy new or unique social situations.
31.	I try not to waste my time on trivial pursuits.
32.	I enjoy caring for my house plants.
33.	I like to keep a daily journal of my daily experiences.
34.	I like to think about numerical issues and examine statistics.
35.	I am good at playing an instrument and singing.
36.	My ability to draw is recognized and complemented by others.
37.	I like being outdoors, enjoy the change in seasons, and look forward to different physical activities each season.
38.	I enjoy complimenting others when they have done well.
39.	I often think about the problems in my community, state, and/or world and what I can do to help rectify any of them.
40.	I enjoy hunting and fishing.
41.	I read and enjoy poetry and occasionally write my own.
42.	I seem to understand things around me through a mathematical sense.
43.	I can remember the tune of a song when asked.

Figure 1.2   Intelligence Assessment. *Source:* Dr. Terry Armstrong.

44. I can easily duplicate color, form, shading, and texture in my work.
45. I like the excitement of personal and team competition.
46. I am quick to sense in others dishonesty and desire to control me.
47. I am always totally honest with myself.
48. I enjoy hiking in natural places.
49. I talk a lot and enjoy telling stories.
50. I enjoy doing puzzles.
51. I take pride in my musical accomplishments.
52. Seeing things in three dimensions is easy for me, and I like to make things in three dimensions.
53. I like to move around a lot.
54. I feel safe when I am with strangers.
55. I enjoy being alone and thinking about my life and myself.
56. I look forward to visiting the zoo.

Figure 1.2 (*Continued*).

SIX THINKING HATS

What Is Six Thinking Hats?

Six Thinking Hats is a strategy developed by Edward DeBono and used in classrooms to help students look at issues from many perspectives. Six different colored hats refer to different ways of examining a problem or issue as seen in figure 1.3.

Examples of Six Thinking Hats:

- Science teacher has students look at cloning from the six hat perspective.
- Social studies teacher has students look at the conflict in the Middle East.
- Students in a health class look at the issue of using steroids for athletic performance.
- Art students examine impressionist paintings from the six hat perspective.
- A disciplinary case in which students reflect on behavior from the six hats perspectives.

Why Use Six Thinking Hats?

Students typically react to a controversial issue viscerally and emotionally, which is red hat thinking. The six hat strategy requires them to use other ways of thinking about problems and issues. It encourages thinking factually, flexibly, logically, creatively, holistically, and heuristically.

Edward DeBono's Six Hat Thinking

White Hat Thinking

Used to think about facts, figures, and objective information.
Symbol: A scientists lab coat
Questions: What are the facts? How did i get them?

Red Hat Thinking

Used to elicit feelings and emotions
Symbol: A heart
Questions: How do i really feel? What is my gut reaction?

Black Hat Thinking

Used to inspire logical, negative arguments - devil's advocate
Symbol: a judge's robe
Questions: What are the possible downside risks and problems?

Yellow Hat Thinking

Used to see the positive outlook - sees opportunities and benefits
Symbol: The warming sun
Questions: What are the advantages? What is the best possible outcome?

Blue Hat Thinking

Used to state the overreaching idea or gist of the situation
Symbol: The sky
Questions: What have I learned? What is the main idea?

Green Hat Thinking

Used to find creative new ideas
Symbol: New shoots sprouting from seeds
Questions: What are some new innovative solutions? How can I see the problem in a new way?

Figure 1.3 Six Thinking Hats. *Source:* DeBono, E. (1999). *Six thinking hats.* Boston: Little, Brown.

Where Would a Teacher Use Six Thinking Hats?

A teacher could use the Six Thinking Hats strategy in any class, any grade, and in any situation.

How Does a Teacher Use Six Thinking Hats?

- First, teach students the thinking associated with each of the colors.
- Next, practice with a particular issue using one of the colors. For example, take the issue of computer internet filtering and apply yellow hat thinking. (What are the advantages of filtering?)
- Then, practice with another color on the same issue. For example, use black hat thinking to look at what are the disadvantages of filtering?
- Continue with each of the colors. This will result in spirited discussion and an amazingly comprehensive range of thinking on an important issue.

For More Information

- www.gamos.demon.co.uk/sustainable/hatpap.htm
- www.naturalmaths.com.au/Settings/six_hats.htm

We now have carefully selected what we consider to be energizing strategies to begin an exciting instructional journey for you and your students. These strategies are not presented or prioritized in any particular order.

These are just a sample of the universe of teaching strategies, ones we consider appropriate for education. Each can be adapted, amplified, modified, or reduced to fit your style and situation. At the end of each strategy, there are a few questions about its brain compatibility, and we've provided sources for more information.

INDUCTIVE/DEDUCTIVE THINKING

Have you ever thought about whether you (and also your students) are inductive or deductive thinkers? The old maxim of "you can't see the forest for the trees" is a perfect example. The forest people are deductive thinkers, that is, their thinking is from the general to the specific. The inductive thinkers are "tree" people who think from the specific to the general.

What do we do as teachers? We explain both types of thinking and demonstrate them. In education, we debate over phonics (inductive) and whole language (deductive). There are countless other examples in history, math, and science.

Students are excited to learn about their proclivity of being a tree or a forest person. We need to be aware of helping students think creatively. We must not block students' creativity by saying to them the following:

- That's not the right answer
- That's not logical
- Follow the rules
- Be practical
- To err is wrong
- Play is frivolous
- Avoid ambiguity

Teach with analogues:

- To realize the value of one year, ask a student who failed a grade.
- To realize the value of one month, ask a mother who gave birth to a premature baby.
- To realize the value of one week, ask the editor of a weekly newspaper.
- To realize the value of one hour, ask the lovers who are waiting to meet.
- To realize the value of one minute, ask a person who just missed the train.
- To realize the value of one second, ask a person who just avoided an accident.
- To realize the value of one millisecond, ask the person who won a silver medal in the Olympics.
- How big is 1,000 dollars?
- One million
- One billion—one city block
- One trillion—63 miles
- One thousand $ bills?

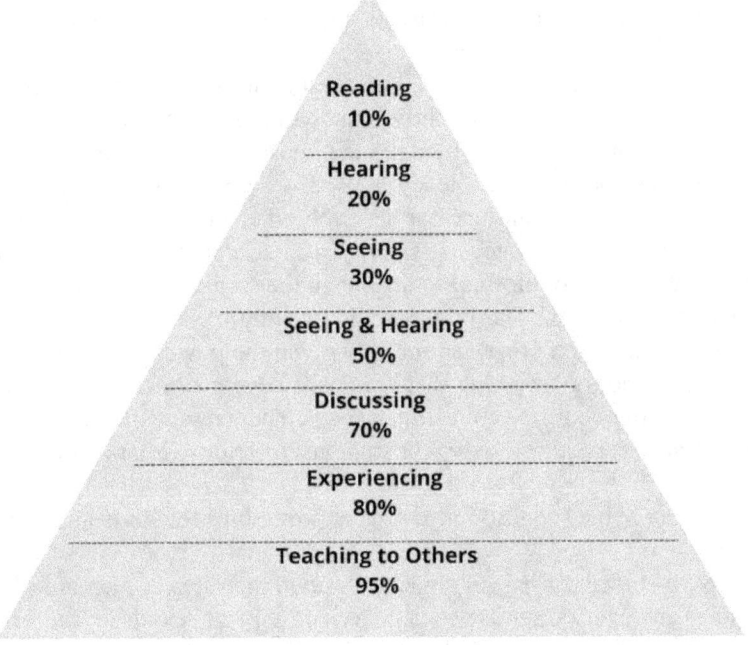

Figure 1.4 Learning Pyramid. *Source:* Wayne Jennings & Joan Caulfield.

We cannot neglect to probe and prod students' thinking. Joan was/is a Spanish teacher. The word for a pen in Spanish is pluma and the word for a pencil is lápiz. When asked how to say pencil in Spanish, a student said lap. Probing him, Joan said, "How did you think of that?" He said "We say pencil. You take away the 'cil' and you have pen. In Spanish you say lápiz so I figured out if you take off 'iz' you say lap." When you think about it, that is good reasoning. Ask students to explain their answers. It can be enlightening. We are sure that you can think of other examples.

We know, as shown in figure 1.4, that only about 20 percent of students learn primarily from books and lectures. This reality leaves 80 percent at various stages of discomfort with schooling delivered in the traditional way. For teachers, the reverse percentages apply. This imbalance puts teachers at odds with many learners and adds to the frustration teachers have working with all students.

Clearly, the learning pyramid, as seen in figure 1.14, shows the efficacy of active learning. The brain thrives on the kind of learning described in the last line on the learning pyramid that most learning comes from what one teaches another. We already know from common observation that children and youth constantly teach each other things, some accurately and some not so accurately. It's pretty well accepted that more learning can be attributed to informal settings than the formal classroom.

Understanding the learning pyramid, we might contrive ways to have students teach each other, particularly given the power of the approach. We should not do anything that we could have a student do—whether writing at the board or collecting papers. The average classroom from third grade on is quite passive for students, a serious violation of student needs.

Here are some suggestions to give opportunities for students to teach:

- Have a student or pair of students explain the rules of the game. This helps any age learner use vocabulary, present, and exercise leadership.
- Have a student explain what went on in class the day before to the returning absent student. It gives the explaining student another opportunity to reflect on and articulate what was covered the day before.
- Use committees, small groups, or task forces to investigate a topic and to teach it to the class. This process can involve high-level skills.
- Have a student handle interruptions of people coming to the room, especially guests. The student manages the interruption and if a visitor, explains what the class is doing and why. One teacher deliberately created interruptions by inviting people to visit often.
- Have students show another student how to use a piece of equipment, such as a computer or audiovisual device.
- Encourage students to become an expert in something so that they can share their knowledge or skills with others.
- Foster sharing and teaching with cooperative learning groups. Sometimes each member develops specialized knowledge that they teach to the others.

Use newspapers, magazines, and other sources such as the internet, so students can teach others topics they have learned.

A school staff might review its practices to see how many fit our knowledge of the brain and therefore should be continued or enhanced, for example, how active the learning is for students.

They might check to see what practices do not fit with current knowledge about the brain and therefore should be discontinued.

Finally, staff might devise what new practices need to be initiated. Among these might entail having students learn more according to the

---

Reflection Sheet

A plan for: _____ Date: _____

What did I choose to do?

What virtues did I forget?

Virtues:

- Honesty
- Compassion
- Courage
- Self-Discipline
- Respect
- Responsibility
- Perseverance

Whom or what did my actions help or hurt?

To be responsible, I must not:

To end this problem, my plan is to:

_____

_____

_____

My Signature: _____

Parent's signature: _____

Teachers signature: _____

Figure 1.5 Reflection Sheet. *Source:* Wayne Jennings & Joan Caulfield.

learning pyramid. This means more learning experiences of an active, hands-on, experiential nature. It's the way our brains take in and process information to build patterns and programs.

Base your classroom rules on an agreed-upon set of values and allow the students to think through their behavior. Consider using the following reflection sheet as shown in figure 1.5.

Take a moment now to reflect on the value of incorporating Inductive/Deductive Thinking in your classroom. Place an X by your level of confidence evaluating its appropriateness for your classroom practice.

1   2   3   4   5   6   7   8   9   10

GRAPHIC ORGANIZERS

Graphic organizers provide ways for students to express their ideas and to promote critical thinking skills. It takes many forms as evident from the examples and cited references.

All stages of learning can benefit from the use of graphic organizers including concept development to presentations.

Graphic organizers can be presented conceptually, hierarchically, sequentially, and cyclically. For example, sequential organizers can be used for timelines (e.g., history), ages (e.g., child development), degrees of something (weight), or rating scales (achievement in school); a cyclical organizer shows how events work together to predict repeated results such as the balance of nature or a cycle of economic changes.

Various software programs allow for easy creation of graphic organizers and allow for editing by individual students or within-group projects. Following are a scant representation of the many forms this useful strategy takes.

Examples of Graphic Organizers

The examples as seen in figures 1.6 through 1.12 have been created and used by Amy Reilly and Jo McFadden, secondary school teachers in Hutchinson, Kansas.

The graphic organizer (figure 1.13), for example, is a concept map developed by a team of teachers in Minneapolis at Marcy School. The map illustrates how to plan an environmental studies unit that includes planning, implementing, and evaluating an extended winter camping experience.

Stair Climbing

Climb the stairs towards the given goal

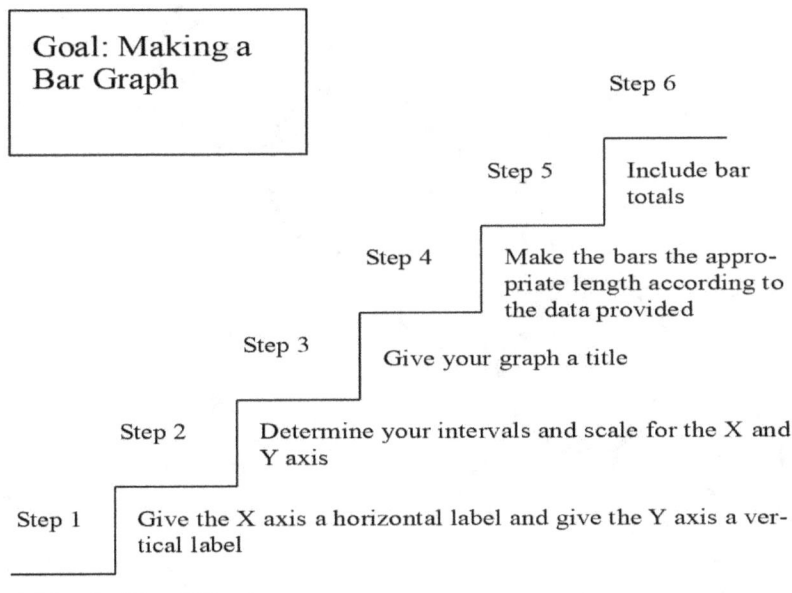

Figure 1.6 Graphic Organizer: Stair Climbing. *Source:* Amy Reilly and Jo McFadden.

Why Use Graphic Organizers?

As Dunston has pointed out, graphic organizers help students integrate prior knowledge with new learning and see relationships between concepts.[3] It provides varied visual learning to meet differences in learning styles and multiple intelligences.

Where Would a Teacher Use a Graphic Organizer?

- To focus attention
- To organize complexity

Chapter 1

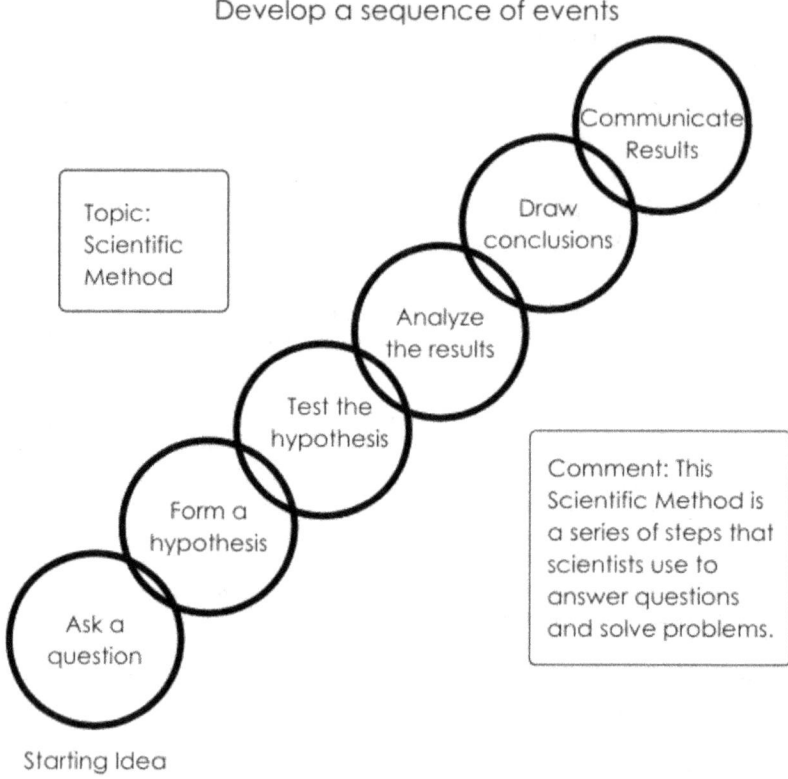

Figure 1.7 Graphic Organizer: Chain Link. *Source:* Amy Reilly and Jo McFadden.

- To enhance concept understanding
- To introduce a new unit or topic
- To prepare for prewriting
- To connect seemingly disparate facts and information

How Does a Teacher Use a Graphic Organizer?
- Provide a graphic organizer template for students to complete.
- Have students create their own graphic organizer to demonstrate learnings.
- Use appropriate software to create mind maps and graphic organizers.

Compare/Contrast

Contrast two ideas at the top and at the bottom. Put similarities in the middle.

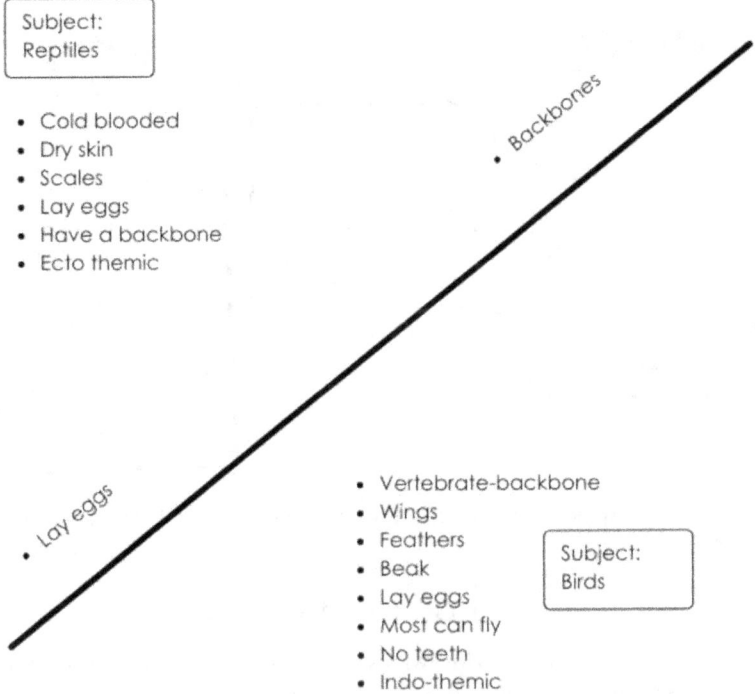

Figure 1.8 Graphic Organizer: Compare/Contrast. *Source:* Amy Reilly and Jo McFadden.

For More Information

- www.ncrel.org/sdrs/areas/issues/students/learning/lr2refer.htm
- www.teach-nology.com/web_tools/graphic_org/
- www.graphic.org/links.html

Take a moment now to reflect on the value of Graphic Organizers in your classroom. Place an X by your level of confidence evaluating its appropriateness for your classroom practice.

1   2   3   4   5   6   7   8   9   10

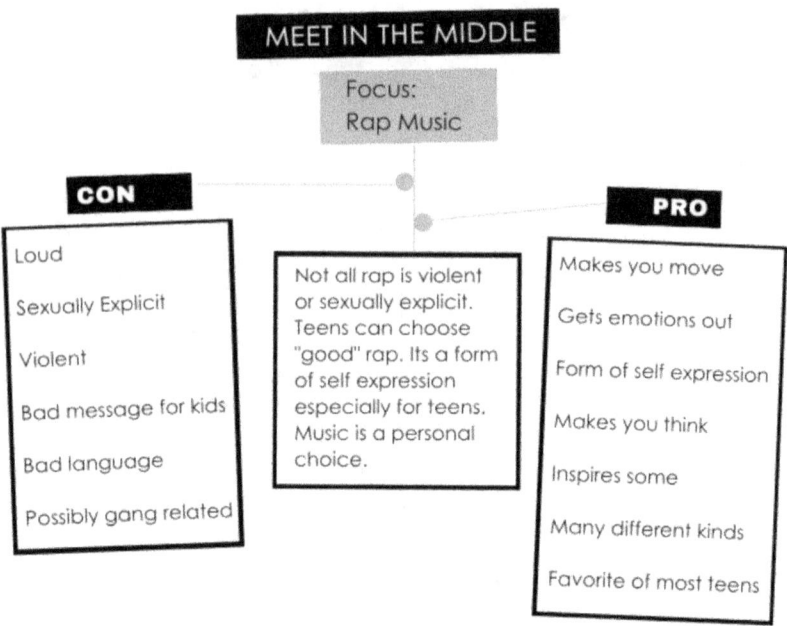

Figure 1.9   Graphic Organizer: Meet in the Middle. *Source:* Amy Reilly and Jo McFadden.

CHOICE BOARDS

Use of Choice Boards (also known as tic-tac-toe or think-tac-toe) enables students to choose tasks to practice a skill or demonstrate and extend understanding of a process or concept. It is an excellent example of the application of Bloom's Taxonomy. From the board, students choose (or teacher assigns) three adjacent or diagonal tasks to complete tic-tac-toe.

Examples of Choice Boards:

These examples of Choice Boards provide models for easy reference. Teachers can adapt the models for myriad lessons and project needs.

Why Use Choice Boards?

Choice Boards provide an effective way to differentiate instruction for interests or readiness levels. It honors student options, thereby increasing motivation. Tasks can be tiered for differing abilities. Experience shows that students love this activity for its choices and freedom to work individually or in groups.

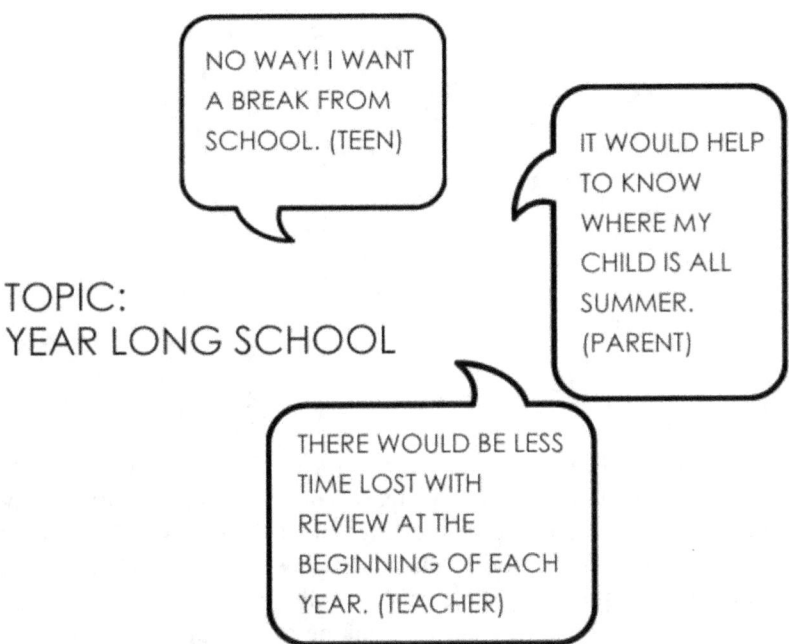

Figure 1.10 Graphic Organizer: Bubble Quotes. *Source:* Amy Reilly and Jo McFadden.

Where Would a Teacher Use Choice Boards?

Choice Boards are adaptable for use in any subject area.

How Does a Teacher Use Choice Boards?

- Identify the outcomes and instructional focus using Bloom's *Taxonomy of Educational Objectives, Handbook 1: Cognitive Domain* and student interest.
- Design nine to sixteen different tasks.
- Write the tasks, one task to each square on a tic-tac-toe board.

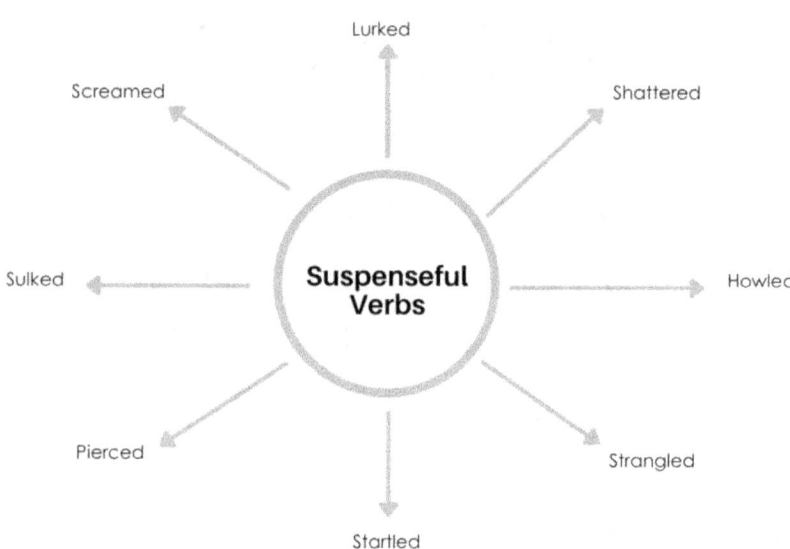

Figure 1.11 Graphic Organizer: Web. *Source:* Amy Reilly and Jo McFadden.

- You may want to select one critical task to place in the center of the board for all students to complete, or you may decide to arrange the tasks in rows according to the level of difficulty. A better way to arrange the tasks is to follow the model above so that no matter which direction the student completes the straight line, at least one of the tasks will include a higher-level thinking skill of analysis, synthesis, or evaluation.
- Choose activities in a tic-tac-toe design. Students form tic-tac-toe horizontally, vertically, diagonally, or in the four corners. They may decide to be finished or to keep going and complete more activities.
- Students can make a star by the activities they plan to complete—in effect, a learning contract—and shade in the box when they finish an activity.
- Teachers can furnish feedback to the student and assess both qualitatively according to a predetermined rubric and quantitatively per standards.

Take a moment now to reflect on the value of incorporating Choice Boards in your classroom. Place an X by your level of confidence evaluating its appropriateness for your classroom practice.

1   2   3   4   5   6   7   8   9   10

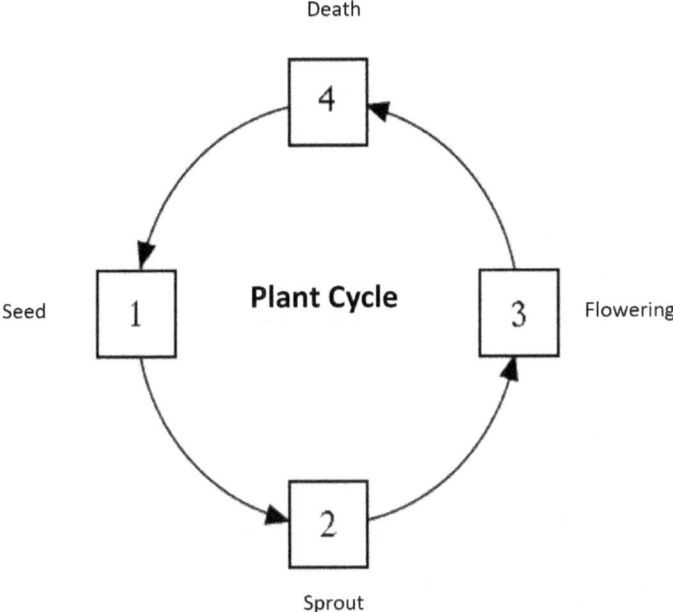

Figure 1.12 **Graphic Organizer: Cyclical Web.** *Source:* Amy Reilly and Jo McFadden.

CUBING

Cubing is a strategy of differentiating or individualizing instruction to help students think at their readiness and interest level about a topic from six perspectives, as shown in figures 1.14 and 1.14b. Cubing refers to a six-sided cube on which questions are written by the teacher or the student on each side of the cube. An example is seen in figure 1.15. Bloom's taxonomy furnishes a template for the questions.

Examples of Cubing

- In English class, students choose from among several cubes each with different levels of difficulty to complete tasks, each of which is written on each side of the cube.
- Science students study the respiration system through tasks written on each side of the cube.
- Music students study composers of the jazz age by demonstrating the different types of beat and rhythm from each side of the cube.

22   *Chapter 1*

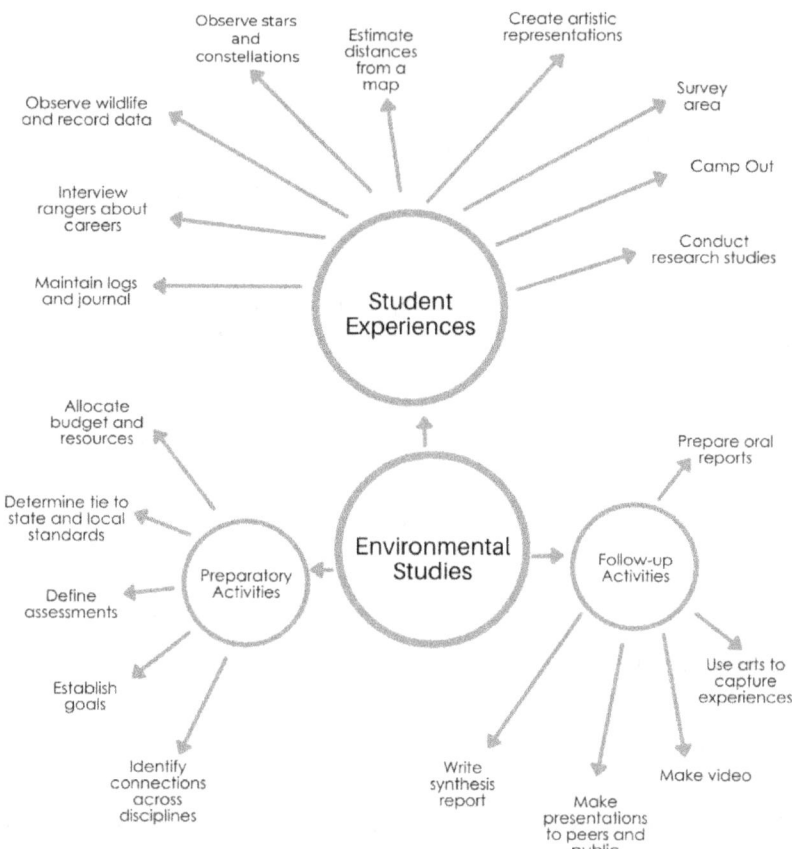

Figure 1.13 Graphic Organizer: Web of Environmental Studies. *Source:* Marcy School.

One example of a cube comes from differentiated instruction and is called a tiered cube. The tiers refer to levels of difficulty. Think of stair steps where each step takes you to a higher position as seen in figure 1.16. Tiered instruction moves students from easier to more challenging levels based on such factors as readiness, past performance, interest, and talent.

The drawing, figure 1.17, using the example of *Light in the Forest* by Conrad Richter, represents three different cubes. Reading vertically yields one at one set level of difficulty. Read horizontally to see how

Mastering the Power of Thinking

Collect	Teach	Draw	Judge
facts or ideas which are important to you.	a lesson about your topic to our class. Include at least one visual aid.	a diagram, map or picture of your topic.	two different viewpoints about an issue. Explain your decision.
(Knowledge)	(Synthesis)	(Application)	(Evaluation)
Photograph	Demonstrate	Graph	Create
videotape, or film part of your presentation.	something to show what you have learned.	some part of your study to show how many or how few.	an original home, dance, picture, song, or story. Elaborate. (Synthesis)
(Synthesis)	(Application)	(Analysis)	
Dramatize	Survey	Forecast	Build
something to show what you have learned.	others to learn their opinions about some fact idea or feature of your study. (Analysis)	how your topic will change in the next 10 years.	a model or diorama to illustrate what you have learned.
(Synthesis)		(Synthesis)	(Application)
Create	Memorize	Write	Compare
an original game using the facts you have learned.	and recite a quote or a short list of facts about your topic. (Knowledge)	an editorial for the student newspaper or drawn an editorial cartoon.	two things from your study. Look for ways they are alike and different.
(Synthesis)		(Evaluation)	(Analysis)

Figure 1.14a Generic Choice Board (Use Your Own Subject Matter). *Source:* Bloom, B. (1984). *Taxonomy of educational objectives, handbook 1: Cognitive domain.* Upper Sattle River, NJ: Addison-Wesley.

Sketch a political cartoon to express your opinion about the issue you have selected. Be sure to use irony to make your point. Give your cartoon a caption.	Write, shoot and edit a short video showing your position on the issue you have selected. Be sure that both the video and audio portions of your production use persuasive strategies to imply your position clearly and forcefully. (You may select this option instead of any to the left)	Write and deliver a 3-4 minute persuasive speech arguing your position on the issue you have selected. Be sure to develop an interesting opening and a strong close. Use persuasive strategies to develop your argument, including facts, statistics, and appeals to the audience's emotions and ethics.
Create a poster or posters for a public service announcement related to the issue you have selected. Use your visual design and several persuasive strategies to convince people to agree with your position on the issue.	Using both print and non-print sources, find out as much as you can about this issue. Write a bibliography of all sources you use to research this issue. Turn in all of your notes and highlighted copies of information.	Write an outline of a report stating your position on the issue you have selected and showing the information you have found. Begin your outline with a paragraph stating your position, then use different headings to show your information in outline form. Include a concluding paragraph.
Design several line or bar graphs, pie charts, or tables showing information related to the issue you have selected. You may use a combination of these types of visuals; be sure to label them clearly. Keep in mind that the way information is presented can be a powerful persuasive tool.	Write a two-column script for a political advertisement supporting your position on the issue you have selected. Be sure that both the video and audio portions of your script use persuasive strategies to imply your position clearly and forcefully. (You may select this option instead of any to the right.)	Write a 500-700 word editorial expressing your view on the issue you have chosen. Be sure to use persuasive strategies in your argument, including facts, statistics, and appeals to the reader's emotions and ethics.

Figure 1.14b Choice Board—Using Persuasion to Address a Contemporary Issue. *Source:* Bloom, B. (1984). *Taxonomy of educational objectives, handbook 1: Cognitive domain.* Upper Sattle River, NJ: Addison-Wesley.

the activities address the same objective but increase in difficulty which yields three cubes at different levels.

Why Use Cubing?

Cubing is another way to support both multiple intelligences and Bloom's Taxonomy. It provides novelty and student choice, both appreciated by the brain! It frees the teacher to work with small groups of students.

Where Would a Teacher Use Cubing?

Teachers will find it helpful to use cubing to energize any class.

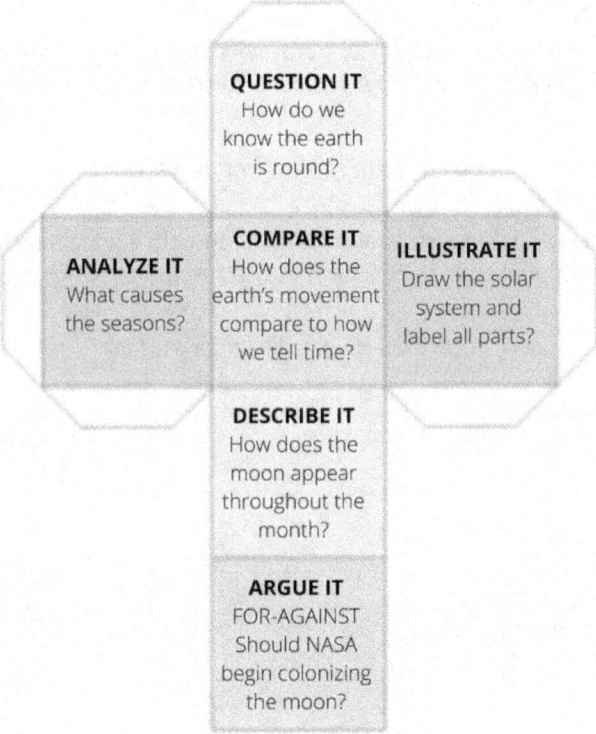

Figure 1.15   Cubing. *Source:* Bloom, B. (1984). *Taxonomy of educational objectives, handbook 1: Cognitive domain.* Upper Sattle River, NJ: Addison-Wesley.

How Does a Teacher Use Cubing?

- Make a cardboard cube. The cube tissue box works well covered with plain paper.
- Write on each side such keywords as the following: Draw a mind map, Argue for, Debate, Question, Sequence, Explain, Prepare, Analyze, Design, Build, Write.
- Determine a topic from your subject, which lends itself to multiple activities.
- Students can work on cubes individually or in groups.
- Toss the cube to a student. Wherever the student's right thumb grasps the cube is the assigned task.
- Then the cube is tossed to another individual or group.

For More Information

- www.bsu.edu/teachers/services/ctr/javits/Instruction/Cubing.htm
- www.mcps.k12.md.us/departments/eii/diffexemplaryex.html#Cubing

STRUCTURED NOTE-TAKING

Structured note-taking is using a template to help students process what they hear and make sense of their notes. It resembles forms, as shown in

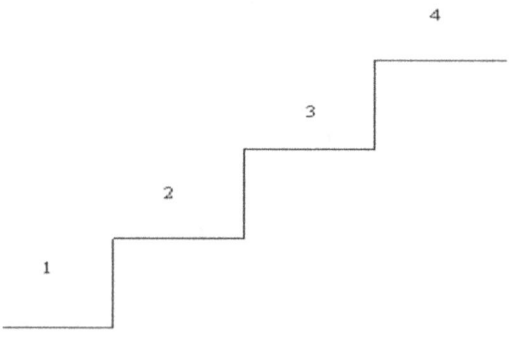

Figure 1.16 Stairs. *Source:* Bloom, B. (1984). *Taxonomy of educational objectives, handbook 1: Cognitive domain.* Upper Sattle River, NJ: Addison-Wesley.

Cube 1: Less Challenging	Cube 2: More Challenging	Cube 3: Most Challenging
Side One On the map provided locate the colonial settlement and the Native American settlement. Represent the topography and river systems. If you wish, make a drawing of the two settlements.	**Side One** Make a chart that contrasts the way in which Native Americans interact with their environments versus the way the white people interact with their environment by using clear examples from the book.	**Side One** Write a paragraph or a poem that contrasts how the two cultures' attitudes toward nature affect the way they use nature
Side Two Develop a timeline that includes at least 10 important events from the novel. Write a brief explanation for each justifying why you think it is so significant.	**Side Two** Decide what you consider to be the three most important events that lead to the climax of the book. Identify them and explain how they build suspense.	**Side Two** Describe the climax of the novel and explain why the author selected that climax.
Side Three Explain the Native American view of education and then describe the colonists' requirements for education. Point out similarities and or differences.	**Side Three** Make a chart that compares the ways in which the Native Americans raise their children to the colonists' approach to raising their children.	**Side Three** Decide which approach to educating children was the most effective, that of the Native Americans, or that of the colonists. Write a persuasive paragraph defending your position.
Side Four Make two scrolls that contain: 1. The codes and rules by which the Native Americans lived, made decisions, and governed themselves. 2. The codes and rules by which the colonists lived and made decisions.	**Side Four** Describe two major decisions made by the colonists and two made by the Native Americans. Compare the process each group used for making those decisions, including roles played by the leaders in each group and the advantages/disadvantages of each.	**Side Four** Write two fully developed paragraphs explaining your answer to the following two questions: 1. Why did the decision to banish True Son have to be made? 2. Did the Native Americans have true democracy?
Side Five Make a chart that compares the advantages that True Son found about native American life with the disadvantages that he found with colonial life.	**Side Five** If you had written this novel, how would you have ended it? Provide at least two well supported reasons to justify your decision.	**Side Five** You have decided to write a sequel to this novel that describes True Son's life after he was banished. Describe the key aspects of your sequel, providing justificaiton for each.
Side Six Make a visual or a log that shows/describes the most important symbols of the Native American culture and those of the colonial culture. Be prepared to explain why you selected the symbols you show.	**Side Six** Make a graphic representation that shows what the Native American culture valued most and one that shows what the colonists valued most.	**Side Six** Decide whether or not the book's title is appropriate. If necessary change the title and write at least one paragraph justifying your decision.

Figure 1.17   Cubing Levels. *Source:* Bloom, B. (1984). *Taxonomy of educational objectives, handbook 1: Cognitive domain.* Upper Sattle River, NJ: Addison-Wesley.

figures 1.16 and 1.18 provided by the teacher, or by simply drawing a vertical line down the center of the page and placing notes on the left about keywords and main ideas. On the right side, students write details amplifying the concepts on the left side. At the bottom of the page, students write a summary.

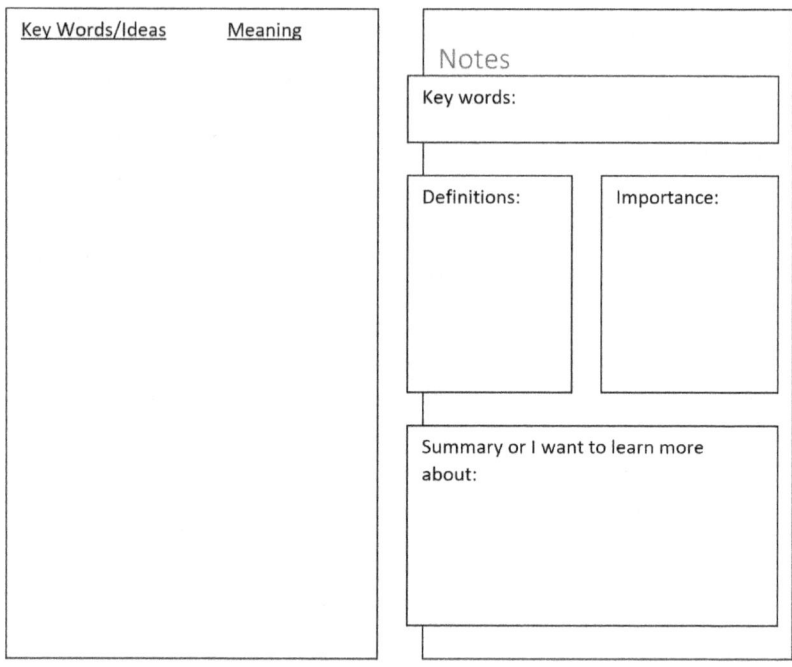

Figure 1.18 Structured Note-Taking. *Source:* Wayne Jennings & Joan Caulfield.

Take a moment now to reflect on the value of incorporating cubing in your classroom. Place an X by your level of confidence evaluating its appropriateness for your classroom practice.

1   2   3   4   5   6   7   8   9   10

Examples of Structured Note-Taking

Structured note-taking is a powerful organizational tool. Students can become immersed in their studies through the process.

Why Use Structured Note-Taking?

As students take notes during a presentation or reading, they have a way to organize their writing. This helps students structure their thinking and leads to greater understanding and reflection on the topic. It makes it easier to review notes and prepare for tests.

Where Would a Teacher Use Structured Note-Taking?

Any class where the teacher expects students to take notes as a way of emphasizing learning or of reinforcing material to be mastered.

How Does a Teacher Use Structured Note-Taking?

- Observe student note-taking and analyze weaknesses.
- Create a template for note-taking that organizes key content.
- Have students practice using the template with easy material.
- Provide templates for students to use thereafter with normal lessons.
- Examine results and show students good examples.

Note: An acclaimed strategy for teachers to use in developing an effective presentation is called the New American Lecture. It offers a comprehensive template for teacher planning but could be adapted for students. See the first website listed in For More Information.

For More Information

- web.odu.edu/webroot/orgs/Educ/Misc/MCTP.nsf/pages/eci795mctp_nalp
- http://www.somers.k12.ny.us/intranet/reading/structuredideas.html
- http://homepage.tinet.ie/~denisdunne1/homework/k05.htm

Take a moment now to reflect on the value of incorporating Note-Taking in your classroom. Place an X by your level of confidence evaluating its appropriateness for your classroom practice.

1   2   3   4   5   6   7   8   9   10

NOMINAL GROUP PROCESS

The nominal group process is a strategy for helping students set goals, define and solve problems, and brainstorm issues. The teacher monitors the discussion, keeps the group working, ensures that everyone participates, and helps the group reach a consensus.

Examples of Nominal Group Process

- Health class discussion of the various dieting methods.
- Students share solutions on funding of presidential elections.
- Students brainstorm ways to get involved in the community.

Why Use Nominal Group Processes?

The nominal group process increases the interaction among students, encourages problem solving, enhances critical thinking, and compares responses with different points of view.

Where Would a Teacher Use Nominal Group Process?

Nominal group processes can be used in any class for discussion of a key question or issue to increase interest and motivation.

How Does a Teacher Use Nominal Group Process?

- Have students write individual responses to the question or problem posed.
- Divide students into teams of four to five members.
- Each group has a leader and recorder.
- In a round-robin fashion, team members share their ideas without comment other than clarification.
- Teams rank-order their ideas.
- Teams share their ideas with other teams.
- Post all ideas on the board.
- Students debate their responses to continue the interaction and learning.

For More Information

- www.extension.iastate.edu/communities/tools/decisions/nominal.html
- www.msue.msu.edu/msue/imp/modii/iii00005.html
- www.oznet.ksu.edu/LEADS/FACT%20Sheets/fact2.pdf

Take a moment now to reflect on the value of incorporating Nominal Group Processes in your classroom. Place an X by your level of confidence evaluating its appropriateness for your classroom practice.

1   2   3   4   5   6   7   8   9   10

THINK-PAIR-SHARE

Think-pair-share (a simpler version of the nominal group process) is a strategy to get students to think about an issue using intrapersonal and interpersonal intelligence. Think-Pair-Share is one of the most common cooperative learning strategies, and it is one of the easiest to use.

Examples of Think-Pair-Share

- In science class: How can our school be more environmentally conscious?
- In math: List as many geometric applications used in building the school?
- In ELL: What challenges are faced by underrepresented cultures in the United States?

Why Use Think-Pair-Share?

The structure is extremely versatile because it can be used for higher-level thinking, as well as basic review and recall.

- All students are involved. As figure 1.19 illustrates, all groups can work together.
- Any student may feel rewarded by seeing their idea emerge in the final version.
- This strategy can be used on the spur of the moment and is non-threatening.
- Discussion of an idea with a partner helps clarify or correct ideas and thinking.

Figure 1.19 Taryn Washington and Addison Funk. *Source:* Photography by Beth Bryant. Image rights—Pembroke Hill.

Where Would a Teacher Use Think-Pair-Share?

A teacher can use think-pair-share in any class to facilitate discussion of ideas.

How Does a Teacher Use Think-Pair-Share?

- Teacher states the issue or problem.
- Each student writes down an idea or two.
- Students tell their ideas to their partners.
- Students listen attentively to their partner's ideas.
- Partners switch roles.
- Class discussion of the ideas from partners.

Take a moment now to reflect on the value of incorporating Think-Pair-Share in your classroom. Place an X by your level of confidence evaluating its appropriateness for your classroom practice.

       1   2   3   4   5   6   7   8   9   10

MENTAL IMAGING

Mental imaging is creating a picture in the mind of the steps to complete a task at hand. Students mentally run through the task performing it perfectly in their mind and feeling great satisfaction.

Examples of Mental Imaging
- Science students mentally practice the steps of dissecting a frog.
- Spanish students mentally practice visiting and ordering a meal at a restaurant.
- Basketball players mentally practice free throws.
- Practical arts students mentally practice the actions of using tools.
- Art students creating their product in their minds before the actual activity.

Why Use Mental Imaging?
Psychologically, learners will tend to be more successful if they can form a mental image of what they need to do.

Successful coaches at all levels use this technique to improve athletic performance.

Where Would a Teacher Use Mental Imaging?
This strategy has application for any subject area. Though seldom used, it has great power to improve performance.

How Does a Teacher Use Mental Imaging?
- Students identify each step and label each step of the task being practiced.
- Students form mental pictures of themselves performing each step successfully.
- Students mentally judge each step of the task according to criteria furnished by the teacher.
- At the completion of the task, the student conducts an overall evaluation based on criteria.

- Students must pay particular attention to feelings of satisfaction from perfect mental performance.
- Upon successful mental imaging, students then can physically perform the task in real-time.

For More Information

- www.eteamz.com/baseball/instruction/pitching/clinic.cfm/Mental%20Imaging/
- t4.jordan.k12.ut.us/Balanced_Literacy/Comprehension/cs_mental_imaging.htm

Take a moment now to reflect on the value of incorporating Mental Imaging in your classroom. Place an X by your level of confidence evaluating its appropriateness for your classroom practice.

1   2   3   4   5   6   7   8   9   10

KWHL STRATEGY (SOMETIMES REFERRED TO AS KWHL)

The KWHL strategy aims to help students use the knowledge they have acquired. It is a variation of the well-known strategy known as KWL.

- K stands for what do we Know?
- W for What do we want to find out?
- H for How can I find the information?
- L for what have we Learned?

Examples of KWHL

- Student knowledge and interest in the Civil War.
- Preparation for a new unit on sonnets.
- Seeing what students know about simple equations in math.

Why Use KWHL?

- KWHL, a group instruction technique, serves to activate prior knowledge.
- Brain compatibility comes in by tapping the collective knowledge students have of a concept or topic thus showing students the connections they already have.
- It also exposes misconceptions to more accurately plan and design instruction based on gaps in knowledge.

Where Would a Teacher Use KWHL?

KWHL can be used in any class:

- Prior to instruction on a new topic to learn what students presently know.
- After a unit to assess understanding.

How Does a Teacher Use KWHL?

- The teacher must have clear learning outcomes that are shared with students.
- Teacher records on a chart or board students' responses to the first two questions: What do you already know? And, what do you want to learn? The teacher will often need to ask probing questions as a way to prod students' responses. An alternative is to have student groups record their responses on a handout chart (see below).
- The teacher and students brainstorm about how they will find information.
- The teacher uses this information to design learning experiences.
- At the completion of the unit, students respond to the last question: What have you learned?
- If interest remains, the teacher determines the next steps, resources, and other activities.
- For example, use table 1.1 to set up a study of the solar system.

Table 1.1 KWHL Chart Wayne Jennings & Joan Caulfield

What Do We Already Know?	What Do We Want To Learn?	How Can We Find Info?	What Have We Learned?

For More Information

- www.ncrel.org/sdrs/areas/issues/students/learning/lr1kwlh.htm
- www.ncwiseowl.org/webquest/spider/Spider%20WebQuest%20KWLH%20Handout.html

Take a moment now to reflect on the value of incorporating KWHL in your classroom. Place an X by your level of confidence evaluating its appropriateness for your classroom practice.

1   2   3   4   5   6   7   8   9   10

SOCRATIC SEMINAR

A Socratic Seminar is a dialogue based on a piece of text which addresses a critical question. The dialogue is open-ended. The only rules are courtesy. Socratic Seminar involves opposing views, debating, and persuading. The topic should be one that has no right or wrong answers. Perhaps the most important component of the process is that teachers refrain from talking entirely. The students' voices must guide the conversation.

Examples of Socratic Seminar-Generic Questions

- Does the text agree or disagree with this statement?
- What does the term ___ mean?

- In what ways are ___ and ___ alike and different?
- What might be some other good titles?
- This passage seems to contradict ___ Agree or disagree?
- How does this passage connect to ___ (refer to another passage or text)?
- What are the inferences?
- What are the implications?
- How did you arrive at your view?

Why Use Socratic Seminar?

Students learn to examine ideas rationally, to explore, and process new ideas. It assumes that many people have pieces of answers and can lead to peaceable solutions. Dialogue creates conditions of open-mindedness and an interchange of views and questioning.

Where Would a Teacher Use Socratic Seminar?

Socratic seminars precede discussions in any class dealing with thought-provoking questions.

How Does a Teacher Use Socratic Seminar?

- Assign a piece of text (one to twelve pages) to read and study. Students are encouraged to underline passages, write questions in the margin, and summarize the meaning.
- Arrange students in a circle for good interaction.
- Give students x number (say three) buttons (any token) as a device to ensure that all students have opportunities to participate. Students surrender a button each time they speak.
- Ask a series of questions that give direction to the dialogue. Rephrase questions until they are understood.
- Assure the flow of dialogue with the teacher as a participant.
- Ask questions that allow for a range of answers.
- Allow for conflict or differences of views.
- Examine answers and draw out implications.
- Request reasons for answers.
- Remain open to questions raised by answers.
- Present all sides of an argument.

- Do not insist on a common agreement.
- See the last website below for an excellent rubric for judging students' participation.

For More Information
- www.ncrel.org/sdrs/areas/issues/students/learning/lr2refer.htm
- www.socraticseminars.com/whatare.htm
- www.studyguide.org/socratic_seminar.htm

Take a moment to assess the value of incorporating Socratic Seminar into your classroom:

1 2 3 4 5 6 7 8 9 10

GALLERY WALK

In a gallery walk, students add comments, answers or provide solutions to posed questions or topics written on newsprint mounted on the wall by circulating clockwise around the room. A variation is called Table Talk where students go from table to table.

Examples of Gallery Walk
- Students evaluate peer work after the completion of a project by visiting each project and making written comments and suggestions.
- In social studies, after studying the Great Depression students circulate individually or in groups to respond to such questions as:
  - What was the political climate?
  - What were the living conditions of average citizens?
  - What was the impact on the arts?
  - What happened in other countries?
  - Under what conditions could a depression happen today?

Why Use Gallery Walk?
Gallery walks generate many solutions and answers to questions. It energizes a class and allows for creativity. It lets the teacher see immediately how much students have learned or not learned.

Where Would a Teacher Use Gallery Walk?

Any teacher can use this strategy to introduce a topic or to summarize what was learned.

How Does a Teacher Use Gallery Walk?

- Questions are posed on chart paper (one per sheet) and posted around the room.
- Students in groups write answers or solutions to the question on the newsprint.
- Students rotate clockwise to the next sheet at a given signal.
- When students return to their initial sheet, they organize the information.
- Students report their summaries to the entire group.
- Teachers can build on the reports to summarize or clarify misunderstandings.
- A variation: students write a question on a 5 × 7 card and it circulates around the table with each person adding an answer or solution.

For More Information

- edservices.aea7.k12.ia.us/framework/strategies/
- www.concordhs.com/ateachsite/processing/gallerywalk.pdf
- www.post1.com/home/garytsu/ITLessonProcess.htm

Take a moment now to reflect on the value of incorporating gallery walks in your classroom. Place an X by your level of confidence evaluating its appropriateness for your classroom practice.

1   2   3   4   5   6   7   8   9   10

SQ3R

SQ3R is an enduring strategy for reading in content areas. Francis Robinson, a psychologist, helping military personnel undergoing accelerated university courses, invented SQ3R during World War II, and it worked well. The method still works well, especially for texts one must understand thoroughly and remember completely. With the emphasis on all teachers teaching reading in their content area, this strategy is particularly useful. S stands for *Survey*. Q stands for *Question*. 3R refers to: R for *Read*, R for *Recite*, R for *Review*.

Examples of SQ3R

- Science assigned reading passages on DNA.
- Physical education text on rules of badminton.
- Music background chapter on culture of an era.

Why Use SQ3R?

To increase reading efficiency and comprehension. To give students specific steps that make the text understandable.

Where Would a Teacher Use SQ3R?

A teacher could use SQ3R for any content that invites students to interpret and analyze information.

How Does a Teacher Use SQ3R?

- *Survey*: Students preview the reading assignment by noting headings, introduction, illustrations, and the summary. This gives students a general idea of the material.
- *Question*: Turn the heading or subtitle into a question before reading each section. This gives the student a purpose for reading the material.
- *Read*: The students then read each section to learn answers to their questions. Students can really enjoy reading as shown in figure 1.20.
- *Recite*: After reading each section, students should again review their question from the heading or subtitle and verify their answer by reciting it in their own words. Students may check their notes or under linings.
- *Review*: After finishing the entire assignment, review each of the headings or subtitles and try to remember the answers to their questions.

For More Information

- www.u.arizona.edu/ic/wrightr/other/sq3r.html
- www.accd.edu/sac/history/keller/ACCDitg/SSSQ3R.htm
- www.accessexcellence.org/AE/newatg/Haugen.sq3rplus

Mastering the Power of Thinking 41

Take a moment now to reflect on the value of incorporating SQ3R in your classroom. Place an X by your level of confidence evaluating its appropriateness for your classroom practice.

    1   2   3   4   5   6   7   8   9   10

Learning strategies assume that engaged students will learn more. Obviously, teaching strategies aim for the same result. The difference, though admittedly tenuous, stems from the locus of control, and also from the authors' desire to more clearly delineate between what are essentially teacher-controlled learning activities versus more student-directed activities.

The distinction, though important, may not look that different in terms of classroom practice. Both are student-centered. There is greater overlap than clear differences, as this chapter's learning activities must be selected and ultimately controlled by the teacher.

We offer these learning strategies as a potent addition to the discussion of thinking strategies because they will help spur greater thinking. Be patient with these strategies. Experience how their use will sharpen the teacher's knowledge of what to attend to for greater effectiveness.

Figure 1.20 Olive Thomas and Noah Thomas. *Source:* Photography by Andrea Morales. Image rights—James Thomas.

Any strategy takes time to hone its details. These strategies powerfully focus student learning and energy. The learning strategies can incite motivation and learning.

Several essential questions arise for schools which use practices following the general principles of this chapter. These questions are particularly pertinent given the national movements on standards, testing, and accountability. Critical questions include:

- Will students learn more?
- What will students learn more of?
- What will students learn less of?
- Is that a good trade-off?
- Will students enjoy school more?
- Will students be more engaged?
- Will students be prepared for their roles as citizens, workers, and lifelong learners?
- Will there be fewer destructive and self-defeating behaviors by students?

The answers to these and similar questions can be found in research studies and the practices of a wide variety of schools over many decades. Clearly, it serves no one well if schools cannot obtain affirmative answers to essential questions.

Although beyond the scope of this book to cite extensive data, the reader might review such material from such groups as the National Association for Core Curriculum, the Association for Experiential Education, The Education Trust, The National Board for Professional Teaching Standards, and the results of experimental schools. We believe the practices described in this book are congruent with valid research studies and help assure vital school outcomes.

COMMITTEES AND TASK FORCES

When forming committees and task forces, students are divided into small groups of about four to six members to work on a complex project or task. Primarily, students work at their own pace and direction. A variation of this strategy is the well-known approach, cooperative learning. More detail about cooperative learning will be discussed in the teaming chapter.

Examples of Committees and Task Forces

- A four-student group works for several weeks trying to figure out the causes of welfare. They make a presentation on their findings.
- A small group of students prepares recommendations about problems of drugs in athletics.
- Five students write a skit on the reactions of sodium with other chemicals.

Why use Committees and Task Forces?

Students enjoy working together and gain valuable skills in doing so. For example, students develop leadership skills by sensing directly what works and what does not in assigning and carrying out the subtasks of the larger goal. They learn the important lesson that each person has different skills and talents such as interviewing, writing, illustrating, speaking.

This is great training for how the world conducts itself, such as when work teams and community groups gather information, determine findings, and make recommendations. The engagement of learners in a good working committee is higher than during lectures or class discussions because minds are active and a level of excitement prevails as people dig for information, solve problems, organize ideas, make discoveries, and teach others what they have learned.

Where Would a Teacher Use Committees and Task Forces?

A teacher can use committees and task forces to encourage exploration of complex topics that do not have simple solutions.

How Does a Teacher Use Committees and Task Forces?

Teachers who have tried committees often report that students waste a lot of time, are off-task, shoot the breeze, or that just one or two members do all the work. Without training, lack of focus will occur. Off task behavior also happens if students are not really interested in the topic or it seems like busy work to them.

Here is a suggestion for the problem of unproductive committees. Have students brainstorm (in small groups) a list of what a dysfunctional committee would be like; what would an ineffective committee spend their time doing? How would members act? Then have each of the small groups give their ideas and jot them down on the board.

Have one or two volunteers make a poster of the ideas to post on the wall. Repeat the exercise for what a high performing group would be like. Post the second chart alongside the first. Take time to talk about how the groups did these two simple tasks. Did they discover any talents or how could they have used special abilities, for example, leadership, taking turns, skirting dominating members, writing or drawing skills. These skills need to be built and reviewed from time to time. The processing time will be well spent.

A second suggestion is to avoid having committees do homework type tasks. Students should own the topic. It needs to be of interest. The topic might be one that they had a hand in determining or choosing from a list of topics. Teachers can generate such a list with student input by asking what students know about the unit or want to learn about the topic using the KWHL strategy in the previous chapter.

For More Information

- coe.sdsu.edu/eet/Articles/jigsaw/index.htm

Take a moment to assess the value of incorporating Committees and Task Forces into your classroom:

1   2   3   4   5   6   7   8   9   10

PERSONAL LEARNING PLANS

Teachers face a nearly impossible situation in conventional classrooms in meeting students' needs. Student differences include wide achievement ranges, such as a seventh-grade class ranging seven school years, from third to tenth grades. Also, student interests vary considerably. Some students are interested in the subject content, while others are disinterested with interests in completely different areas such as animals or drama.

Beyond that, learning modalities vary, for example, preferences for learning alone, learning with another person, or with or without music in the background for homework and study time. Teachers try to meet these differences with various teaching techniques and solicit ideas from colleagues, conferences, books, and staff development programs.

Despite valiant efforts, hyped-up instruction doesn't succeed with all students in the standard classroom, as can be seen from outcomes of boredom, dropouts, and discipline problems.

There is an answer.

Personal learning plans (PLP) skirt the teaching dilemma. PLPs support teachers in overcoming problems of student achievement, disengagement, and learning styles. The PLP approach (sometimes referred to as an individualized learning plan or project-based learning) doesn't arise as an obvious answer. Few schools use PLPs because they can require structural changes for their full implementation. Still, every school can accommodate the concept at a productive level.

Establishing a PLP for every student begins with an acceptance of developing competencies for citizenship, careers, and lifelong learning. Schools can start an advisory program as a foundation for creating PLPs. Students often carry out a PLP with the assistance of specialist teachers, community resource people, and others.

Advisory programs are not homerooms for listening to loudspeaker announcements. However, advisors have a brief time each morning, say, ten minutes, to check in their advisees. Some schools make mistakes using a more extended period for such lessons as citizenship, getting along with others, and honesty.

Advisory lessons of this type mean extra preparation for the teacher and a largely meaningless session for advisees. Some schools schedule an extended advisory period once a week. Experienced advisor turn over much of the time to students for planning activities.

The daily brief advisory gives the advisor opportunities to start the day and schedule meetings with advisees to prepare PLPs, review progress, suggest resources, and encourage meeting the completion date. Students may share personal problems with their advisor. Advisers should refer serious issues to the school counselor or social worker.

One secondary school scheduled an hour per day for each teacher/advisor for individual or small group adviser-advisee meetings. In one high school, adding three additional students to all classes enhanced the advisory period. It met with teacher approval. With an advisory period, teachers had one less class preparation per day.

Some say that school counselors should be the ones to work with students to create their PLPs. That plan is unrealistic given the high student to counselor ratio. Advisers take on *part* of the counselors' role as a more effective way to establish PLPs. Advisers see advisees daily, thereby observing unusual conditions by a student. Advisors can serve as liaisons and assist teachers in getting to know their students.

Ordinarily, teachers aim for personalized learning within subjects. For example, during a westward movement unit, students may be given a choice of topics like building or drawing covered wagons, the mistreatment of American Indians, geography, and other topics related to the unit.

The students' choice at the course level shows a much to be applauded movement toward personalized learning but remains teacher-directed. We suggest a greater degree of change labeled as student-directed learning. Here, the adviser and sometimes the parent help the student establish goals and design their individualized learning experiences.

Personalization occurs with recognizing (and prizing) student differences. One student writes with clarity and spirit; another struggle to put thoughts in writing. Another student displays a wide variety of knowledge and skills. One needs help; the other moves far ahead. A PLP overcomes differences. During adviser-advisee meetings, a PLP unfolds based on learning needs and personal interests. The PLP addresses:

- Societal expectations (such as basic skills, understanding much content such as communicable diseases and government operations)
- Basic academic skills (reading, writing, and arithmetic)
- Broad goals (citizenship, careers, lifelong learning, and personal fulfillment)

Advisee goals, societal expectations, basic skills, and board goals of citizenships, career preparation, and lifelong learning establish what students and the adviser determine for the PLP. Many PLPs call for a project, say, interning in the county attorney's office or sewing a skirt. A seemingly odd and off-target example can encompass a wide variety of learning: reading, research, problem solving, science, competencies, and other essential knowledge and skills.

The PLP identifies resources, expected timelines, presentation methods, and how the adviser, student, and parent judge the student's success, whether in school or beyond its walls. Periodic meetings between the adviser and advisee keep the advisee on course and assist with problems.

Using a PLP for learning raises questions about whether the student learns the expected goals listed in a school course. The coverage issue requires faith that learning results from enthusiastic, motivated students working on an area of interest.

Let's take an extreme example. Some students say they don't have any interests, probably thinking the teacher expected her to declare an interest in a school subject.

For instance, Rhonda stated she had no interests despite the adviser's attempts to open a conversation. With a comment about her unusual hair design, Rhonda brightened. The teacher-adviser asked Rhonda if she knew about hair types, training for becoming a hairstylist, types of chemicals used in hair treatment, fashion, and related topics.

Rhonda had some knowledge about these and was interested in learning more about cosmetology. The adviser saw how Rhonda's interests had academic components of reading, writing, interviewing, note-taking, math, research, chemistry, and presentation skills. The adviser helped Rhonda create an ambitious PLP.

Like, but less formal than special-education individual education plans (IEPs), As shown in figure 1.21, PLPs help students set learning targets. The plan includes goals—say, a manageable two or three—and ways of accomplishing them within a reasonable timeline.

Collaboratively written with the student, the PLP may contain specific steps to find, organize, and present information. Students may not be initially impressed with the greater personal responsibility but will come to see its value. The adviser and PLP style fit the concept of teachers as facilitators of learning because of the focus on learning versus teaching.

Student-run parent conferences offer opportunities for students to review their goals and present how completely they met them. At the conference, the goals may be revised or reinforced because of greater relevance to the students' needs.

The adviser meets periodically with each advisee to review, modify, and adjust the learning program—an individualization for each student. For example, one student may have three hours of piano practice each day because of deep interest. (Imagine Mozart as a child attending school and being told to put away the music; it's time for spelling.)

Another may spend most of the day preparing a presentation on eagle migration.

Another has several projects underway, one involving two other students looking at the water system in the area, another the battles of the Civil War, and another focused on persuasive writing. Yet another student may have an internship or engage in a shadow study of a graphic artist.

These examples show the diversity of learning experiences and heady opportunities to make real-life differences in society. The adviser has the authority to approve projects. Student work approval is by the teacher of record (the licensed teacher with appropriate credentials) for meeting standards.

Choice of projects by the student with the adviser's approval increases motivation and energy to make the learning process work more effectively. PLPs should state the student's strengths, limitations, learning preferences, project description with its datelines, and how the plan is presented. One example of a PLP follows:

PLPs contain directions to shape a student's school life. They are similar to IEP used in special education but far less formalistic. They are a brief document (usually, one page or so) listing a student's interest areas, areas of strength, and areas for growth.

Based on these items, they include several goals and ways of accomplishing the goals with a suggested timeline. What makes a PLP work is that it is collaboratively written *with* the student, neither *about* the student nor *for* the student.

Why Use PLPs?

PLPs make the teacher and the school more aware of student interests and needs. More importantly, the teacher learns of the student's goals and plans. Instructional activities are more easily tailored and more successful if they take account of student interest and well-being.

Where Would a Teacher Use PLPs?

A teacher can use PLPs for any grade level. PLPs work best in elementary schools with a self-contained classroom system and in secondary schools with strong adviser-advisee programs.

Personal Learning Plan

Date_____ Name_____
Teacher-Advisor_____

What do you enjoy doing outside of school?

If you were given the chance to change anything in your neighborhood, what would you change and why?

Who do you consider a role model in your life and why?

If given the opportunity to go anywhere in the world, where would you choose to go? What would you do while you were there?

What are your personal strengths? What do you do best?

What areas do you think could use improvement?

In which of the following ways do you learn best? You can check more than one.
- ☐ Verbal—words, listening, talking, discussing, reading
- ☐ Logical—puzzles, problems, numbers, math
- ☐ Spatial—visual pictures, art, hands-on activities, fixing things
- ☐ Musical—music, hearing, lyrics, sounds
- ☐ Body—movements, using your hands, activities
- ☐ Interpersonal—working with people, team activities
- ☐ Intrapersonal—working alone, reflecting, self-motivated
- ☐ Natural—nature, plants, animals, outdoors

What top goals do you want to work on?

What is the project you plan to work on?

What resources will you use?

When will you be ready to present your project?

What do you want to do/ achieve after graduation?

Advisor comment:
Parent comment:
Student comment:

We, the undersigned, commit to the success of this plan.

Student Signature_____ Parent Signature_____

Teacher-Advisor Signature_____

Figure 1.21 Personal Learning Plan. *Source:* Joan Caulfield & Wayne Jennings.

How Does a Teacher Use PLPs?

It is best if an entire school adopts a program of PLPs. That means establishing times for parent-student-teacher/adviser conferences. Ideally, conferences would be held at the beginning of year—actually just before the first day of school. Such conferences, successfully run, will have a thoughtful discussion while completing the PLP form.

Subsequent conferences during the year and at the end of the year are used to review the personal learning form for progress and to determine if modifications are necessary. We have found that progress conferences are best if student-led.

Teachers should allow their students to report on their progress and make them accountable for progress with their learning plans. Students can be helped in this process with a brief rehearsal, and in time they will become quite adept at describing their progress, clarifying their goals, and establishing more specific and appropriate goals.

For More Information

- www.bigpicture.org/MetPort96-7personalizedLearning.htm

LEADERSHIP CAMPS

A leadership camp generally occurs in an off-school setting or if in school, a non-classroom setting such as the gym. Camp implies an informal environment with an extended setting, for example, sitting on the ground or the floor, or in a circle with activities over several days. Leadership camps need skilled adults for conducting activities with gusto and excitement.

Examples of Leadership Camps

- Student councils use leadership camps to generate spirit, teamwork, and motivation to help make their school the best it can be.
- An interdisciplinary team of four teachers and their 100 students go to a retreat to work out details of how the group can have an extraordinary year.
- At a retreat setting, students and staff are trained to establish a peer counseling program for their school.

Figure 1.22 Saige Wimes, Josie Wissel, and Sofia Stockwood. *Source:* Photography by Doug Hesse. Image rights—STA.

Why Use Leadership Camps?

Use leadership camps to build spirit, to generate energy, and to break the mold of student passivity. Students have great reserves of learning power and drive that can be awakened and revitalized. The nontraditional setting, energizing activities, and high degree of active participation lift students from lethargy to new levels of vigor and interest.

Where Would a Teacher Use A Leadership Camp?

An individual class might go into "camp" mode to settle serious structure problems of disinterest or dysfunction. The normal operating mode would be suspended to address critical issues for success. As shown in figure 1.22, students enjoy being outside of the classroom. Any class or program might profit from such an activity.

How Does a Teacher Use a Leadership Camp?

The leadership camp strategy requires much planning. It is probably best planned with a team from the staff working with a skilled facilitator. Experienced student council advisers are familiar with camps.

School administration needs to provide support and clear obstacles, especially if other classes are in session at the same time.

For More Information

- www.principals.org/pdf/nlc_2004brochure.pdf
- www.nhs.us/pdf/nslc04_adultstaffapp.doc
- media3.iss.indiana.edu/htbin/wwform/www/?TEXT=R18279575-18283259-/www/documents/188/cat/wwi770.htm

ROLE-PLAYING

Role-playing is simulating a person or situation so that it can be examined, analyzed, and is better understood.

Examples of Role-Playing

- Students make a skit of how it feels to be ignored.
- A student takes the role of Douglas Macarthur on hearing he has been relieved of his command by the President of the United States.
- Students practice their part in the upcoming parent-student-adviser conferences in which each will lead the session.

Why Use Role-Playing?

Role-playing is one of the most engaging activities as the entire group will watch and analyze the role play with great interest. They mentally play the same role and think how they might have handled the situation. They quickly identify with an issue because the role play almost automatically draws them in whether as one of the players or onlookers. Students get "outside" of themselves to look at a situation with lessened fear or embarrassment since they are not technically being themselves, but just playing a role. Students enjoy watching other students.

Where Would a Teacher Use Role-Playing?

Any class can use skits or dramatic incidents to reinforce or deepen learning.

How Does a Teacher Use Role-Playing?

A teacher may ask, for example, how you think the character in a novel (or with a current event) might have handled the situation differently. Rather than just discussion, ask who would like to take the part of the characters and play it out differently. You could combine role-playing with committees and have each group come up with a skit or interpretation.

COMMUNITY SERVICE

Community service, often referred to as service learning, is the placing of students in community agencies, businesses, schools, or other situations beyond the school's operation so that students learn by direct participation about how aspects of the world function.

Examples of Community Service

- Students tutor younger students at a nearby elementary school.
- Students serve a few hours a week at locales such as hospitals, shelters, and fish hatcheries.
- Students shovel snow or mow lawns for the elderly near the school.

Why Use Community Service?

Placement where students assume responsibility in real-world settings teaches responsibility, how adults function, and how important tasks are fulfilled. They begin to understand how their skills, interests, and inclinations will serve them in the future. They see directly that work is largely without the glamorization and unrealistic degree of excitement television portrays. Career aspirations may be formed and perhaps some lines of work will be found uninteresting—and important outcome.

Where Would a Teacher Use Community Service?

Any class, for example, a math teacher might have students spend some time in architect or engineers' offices, or carpenter job sites to see the application of math to life. Use community service to bring reality and life to school subjects.

How Does a Teacher Use Community Service?

Community service requires schedule flexibility. It would be impossible to go from third period to a site a mile from school, have significant participation at the site, and make it back to school for fourth-hour class. Some traditionally scheduled schools arrange for community service at the beginning or end of the day by using some school time and some student personal time. Other schools establish schedules that permit leaving classes once a week, say, Wednesday afternoons. Some schools employ a person to assist teachers in community placements.

It is best to place students in situations where the interest of the student is greatest. Some states mandate a certain number of hours of community service for graduation in the same manner traditional subjects are required. Give "credit" for community service. That recognizes the essential value of the program.

Students involved in community service need opportunities to debrief and reflect on their experiences in order to obtain maximum benefit from their service. They can remark on critical questions such as: what made the experience good (or poor)? Could they have made it better? How effectively did they interact with adults in situations? What makes a good worker at their service site? What key lessons were learned from the community service experience?

For More Information

- www.servicelearning.org/

EXCHANGES

Exchanges involve spending time in another setting such as between two schools or in another community or country.

Examples of Exchanges

- Students from urban schools spend two weeks in a rural school and vice versa.
- Students have year-long exchanges between countries for individual students.
- Students spend a day in a school across town with different demographics.

Why Use Exchanges?

Exchanges expose students to new settings and interrupt stereotypic thinking. Students come to see and understand people they previously didn't know and for whom they may have had incorrect notions. They see similarities among people's issues. They begin to understand another cultural setting. Exchanges can be among the most important experiences a student will have in school.

Where Would a Teacher Use Exchanges?

Teachers use exchanges to deepen understanding of other cultures by taking students from the known and comfortable environs of their own culture and immersing them into another cultural situation thus requiring adapting to new conditions.

How Does a Teacher Use Exchanges?

While exchanges pay off in student understandings of other points of view, they require a great deal of preparation ranging from simple one-day exchanges with another school and those involving, say, two weeks in another city.

First, the teacher must be clear about the purposes of the exchange and be able to communicate the purposes with students and their parents. Exchanges involving several days to weeks should be done one school at a time, that is, one school does the exchange and later the other school does the return exchange. Such exchanges require written permission from parents.

Paperwork includes such information as medical conditions, medical contacts, permission to take medical action in an emergency if parents are not reachable, and notice that students will be sent home at parent's expense if serious disciplinary problems arise. When students stay with other families, the receiving school approves the family's participation. Food and costs are borne by the receiving family, except for transportation to the site. Students attend the other school just as they would their own school. School administration and school board approval are essential to success and legal requirements.

For More Information

- www.yfu-usa.org
- www.nwse.com
- www.afs.org

CLASS MEETINGS

Class meetings are when the entire class goes into "executive session" to make important decisions. The meeting is best run by student officers who have been elected and each student has an opportunity to propose actions, talk for or against proposals, and vote on their disposition. Class meetings are run by the rules of parliamentary procedure or other established rules, thus ensuring that each person has equal rights and equal opportunities to participate.

Examples of Class Meetings

- A class decides on which of several field trips will best serve their learning.
- A class establishes committees to study a current problem and make recommendations.
- A class makes recommendations for future topics of study.
- Some schools use meetings to handle infractions of rules established by the students or school.

Why Use Class Meetings?

- Class meetings are exercises in democracy.
- Students learn how decisions are made and each person's critical role in influencing the outcomes of decisions.
- Students come to better understand fellow students' reasoning and positions.
- Students sharpen critical thinking skills.
- Students learn to organize and present their thoughts.
- Students learn how organizations make decisions.
- Students learn the essentials of parliamentary procedures so that they will feel comfortable and competent in their roles as members of boards and committees in organizations.

Where Would a Teacher Use Class Meetings?

The most common use is in English and social studies classes where the subject matter is about civics, speaking, and correct procedures. Still, this doesn't preclude their use in a less formalistic way in other settings. The teachers do not concentrate as much attention on Roberts Rules of Order.

How Does a Teacher Use Class Meetings?

Begin by talking with students about your willingness to share important decisions about future actions. The teacher should be clear about her ultimate veto power of decisions that are illegal or inappropriate for the subject matter of the class. Nonetheless, that leaves considerable decision-making capacity for the students as a group.

Students will find learning the basics of parliamentary procedure a bit frustrating, but that stage doesn't last long and they come to greatly enjoy the process because there is fair treatment of each person. They need to learn that each person is equal, meaning that each has an equal opportunity to propose ideas, participate in discussion of ideas, and vote on their implementation. The basics of parliamentary procedure include:

- How to make a motion.
- Seconding a motion.
- Discussion of a motion.
- Voting on a motion.
- The role of the chairperson or president.
- The importance of an accurate record of the proceedings.
- The responsibilities of officers and how to select them.
- How effective committees are selected and operate.

As students learn the basics, they come to relish class meetings. They will ask when the next meeting will occur and rarely will be absent for it. This takes several meetings before this state of mind arrives but it has great payoffs in student morale and learning.

For More Information

- www.ncrel.org/sdrs/areas/rpl_esys/collab.htm
- www.stenhouse.com/pdfs/8134fm.pdf

SPARKS

Sparks is a term devised by Leslie Hart, a pioneer in brain-based learning.[4] He used it to describe activities that created a spark of interest in learning more about a topic. Hart proposed that schools should have several sparks a week. There would be speakers, demonstrations, and events mostly outside the customary activities of the school or class.

The old-time school assembly is an example of a spark but has become passé given the power of television to bring the best in the world into every home. Sparks work best in a smaller setting, say, an individual class or two joined classes, where the give and take permits easy exchanges between the presenter and students.

Examples of Sparks

- A parent explains the nature of her job as an attorney.
- A neighbor tells about a trip to Egypt.
- An artist demonstrates the technique of macramé.

- A city council person talks to the class via speaker phone.
- An Indian parent tells about her upbringing.

Why Use Sparks?

Sparks add valuable input to the brain, which is often starved for input in the average classroom. The brain needs input. It is the raw material for the basic building blocks of patterns and programs in the brain. The brain is a remarkable pattern detecting device and will extract meaning from experiences, almost irrespective of their seeming inappropriateness. Sparks provide a new experience for the brain which is most alert at such times, hence the potential for more learning and new connections to previous learnings.

Where Would a Teacher Use Sparks?

A teacher can use Sparks in any class and at any time. Leslie Hart suggested that input to the brain should be increased by a factor of ten in schools. Sparks provide excellent input.

How Does a Teacher Use Sparks?

Interestingly, almost any kind of spark can be used at anytime profitably. Teachers should not worry about whether a given spark will fit the topic under study at the moment. The brain will extract meaning in many ways in response to new sparks. The teacher should be alert to possible sparks.

Some poll parents for people willing to share their experiences, for example, careers, hobbies, travels, interests, illnesses, cooking, skills, talents, history, and so on. The list is endless. The teacher invites the person to the class (several classes might share the experience), has the person describe their interest, and leaves time for interaction with the students.

FIELD TRIPS

Field trips are excursions by a class or small group into the community to learn by direct observation or participation. All schools use field trips but few use them extensively because of the expense and other factors. Still, field trips can be used more widely if done in small groups with proper preparation. A search for material on the web turned up endless references to virtual field trips. This discussion focuses on real field trips.

Examples of Field Trips

- A class attends a concert.
- Three students interview the chief of police about delinquency.
- Two students from a math class visit architectural offices to see applications of geometry.

Why Use Field Trips?

Field trips give students first-hand information, an essential way of learning for their brains. Field trips are examples of complex learning because of their many facets. The planning and debriefing of a field trip with students provides valuable reinforcement of learning crucial knowledge and skills being promoted by a lesson or unit.

Where Would a Teacher Use Field Trips?

Any class benefits from field trips if properly managed. Teachers can efficiently use field trips more often through small groups.

How Does a Teacher Use Field Trips?

As teachers desire other ways of building understanding, they can turn to the strategy of field trips by thinking about resources in the community. Every community has a "goldmine" of resources: people, organizations, places, and events. Consider whether it is feasible for the entire class because of cost, supervision, and scheduling.

Often, an easier way is to send from two to five students. Costs are less, supervision will be replaced by careful advance planning, and scheduling is a matter of school policy that permits students to miss other classes if on a scheduled field trip. Planning includes a form to parents that describes the trip and that the school will not be liable for accidents.

Students need to complete forms showing their route, timetable, who they will meet, where they will meet the resource, and emergency phone information. More importantly, there must be clarity of purpose, relationship of content to the class, clear, clean questions to gather information about, and, if necessary, rehearsals of how to interview, observe, and take notes.

Finally, students need to do something significant with the experience upon return. They should prepare a presentation of key points and be prepared to answer questions. They should also review the process of the trip itself: was the planning adequate, did transportation arrangements work out, was the resource helpful, could students have been better prepared, did everyone cooperate?

These questions add to the learning experience and set the stage for more effective field trips in the future. Figure 1.23 summarizes the planning, execution, and follow up for a field trip.

For More Information

- www.gsn.org/project/fieldtrips
- See also local lists of places, published by the media, chambers of commerce, etc.

Take a moment to assess the value of incorporating field trips into your classroom.

1   2   3   4   5   6   7   8   9   10

LEARNED EXPERTISE

Learned expertise is a program in which students become experts at some area of knowledge.

Examples of Learned Expertise

- Each student becomes an expert about a state.
- Each student becomes an expert about some career area.
- Pairs of students become experts about a form of literature.

> Getting the Most from Field Trips
>
> Before Trip
>
> - Plan with students.
> - Have them share what they know already.
> - Have them visualize what they will see.
> - Make list of questions or things to note.
> - Determine significance of trip to their lives.
> - Use open ended probes: On this trip I expect to learn…I'm looking forward to learning…
>
> During Trip
>
> Review details of the trip:
>
> - How long will you stay?
> - Meeting place?
> - Lost person?
>
> Have Student helpers on the trip:
>
> - Roster keeper
> - Photographer
> - Note taker
> - General assistant
> - Introducer
> - Thank you persons.
>
> Back Home
>
> Much more is gained from debriefing and reflecting on trip:
>
> - Review what was learned.
> - How did trip compare with what they expected?
> - Value of trip?
> - Recommend to others?
> - Any changes?
> - Repeat the trip?
> - Related trips?
> - Plan follow up presentations or reports for students who didn't go and for parents.
> - Send thank-you—students design them, of course.

Figure 1.23   Getting Mileage From Field Trips. *Source:* Wayne Jennings & Joan Caulfield.

Why Use Learned Expertise?

This strategy motivates students particularly when they have a choice of topic. They enjoy becoming the key person who knows a segment of knowledge and shares it with others.

Where Would a Teacher Use Learned Expertise?

A teacher can use learned expertise to delve into any subject.

How Does a Teacher Use Learned Expertise?

- Tell students that they are going to learn a great deal of information about many aspects of a subject, say, trees.
- Each will choose a tree to investigate and become an expert in information about that tree.
- They will need to gather information from a variety of sources.
- At this point, take time to talk about sources on information: internet, library, texts, people, organizations, yellow pages, and so on.
- Students then choose their topic and go to work.
- Depending on student skill levels, you may have to teach note-taking, interviewing, and data organization.
- It is a good idea to require periodic progress reports you do in writing or orally.
- In a final session, they share their learning with the class, or better yet, make presentation boards for parents, the public, or other classes to view and make themselves available to respond to questions.

PUPIL-TEACHER PLANNING

Pupil-teacher planning is the practice of planning content and procedures with students. It has been around for a long time though seldom seen in practice to any major degree. In its pure form, as a means of empowerment, students play major roles in determining the direction and conduct of a class. Few teachers would have the authority or inclination to take it this far, powerful as the strategy is. However, in a more limited way, teachers can very profitably plan aspects of a class with students.

Examples of Pupil-Teacher Planning

- Teachers plan all or most aspects of a field trip *with* students.
- Teachers plan with students what questions the next unit of study in history will cover.
- The teacher offers choices of topics in microbiology.

Why Use Pupil-Teacher Planning?

Empowerment of students through shared decision-making motivates students. It pays a high compliment to students because the teacher regards their ideas as important. The brain thrives on self-determination and teacher approval. Learning accelerates under conditions of empowerment. Pupil-teacher planning is a form of democracy in action.

Where Would a Teacher Use Pupil-Teacher Planning?

A teacher should use pupil-teacher planning with any class where the teacher wishes to increase learner ownership.

How Does a Teacher Use Pupil-Teacher Planning?

At its simplest form, offer choices to the class, for example, about which to do first, what topic to do next, or what form of exam to use. The more classic form involves students listing questions they have about either a topic or more broadly, topics themselves.

A good way to do this is to have students individually jot down their questions, share these in pairs, list them on the chalkboard, and ultimately vote them up or down after listing criteria for making a decision. The decisions are then implemented, perhaps again involving students in the plans for implementation.

For More Information

- www.newhorizons.org/strategies/democratic/kennedy.htm

DAILY NEWSPAPER

The daily newspaper strategy is using the community newspaper in the classroom for extending and amplifying learning.

Examples of the Daily Newspaper Strategy

- Students present items from the newspaper in civics twice a week.
- Students in math class determine batting averages and compare their numbers with statistics from the sports page.

- Students in science examine the weather page for interesting climate data.
- Students use the *Wall Street Journal* to study ideas about economic policy.

Why Use the Daily Newspaper Strategy?

The newspaper reports on reality, thus linking school to the real world. This adds meaning that reinforces and deepens learning. Students may even talk with parents about their newspaper and its connection to school learning. Students take a greater interest in the newspaper and discover many interesting parts of major newspapers. With this knowledge, schoolwork comes more alive and its relevance can be seen.

Where Would a Teacher Use the Daily Newspaper Strategy?

Any class can apply the newspaper as a teaching/learning tool.

How Does a Teacher Use the Daily Newspaper Strategy?

The school should subscribe to a bundle of newspapers. These can be divided among classes or shared on certain days. Most newspaper publishers make classroom sets available at a substantial discount. Students on a rotating basis can be given assignments every day to report on relevant topics, from sports, political cartoons, statistics, science in the news, funnies (don't forget humor in the classroom), want ads, and so on.

These offer opportunities for discussion, questions, follow up, reflection—all resulting in more learning. Some newspapers publish booklets of, say, 100 ways to use the newspaper in the classroom

For More Information

- www.suelebeau.com/nie.htm
- cnnstudentnews.cnn.com/fyi/
- www.eduref.org/cgi-bin/printlessons.cgi/Virtual/Lessons/Language_ Arts/Journalism/JNL0199.html
- Check with your large city newspaper publishers for booklets on using the newspaper in the classroom.

EXHIBITIONS AND PRESENTATIONS

Exhibitions and presentations offer students a chance to show what they have learned in a public setting either in the classroom for peers or in a broader community setting. Students give presentations about a completed project or what they have researched. They may do this in many ways: storyboards, media presentations, drama, speeches, public displays, and so on.

Examples of Exhibitions and Presentations
- Students set up science fair type displays at the mall for the public to view.
- As a culminating activity, students present their future schools projects to another class.
- Students present a skit to the city council on the need for a youth recreation center.
- Students make presentations to other classes or at nearby elementary schools.

Why Use Exhibitions and Presentations?
An exhibition of learning for an audience beyond the teacher motivates students to higher levels of performance. The last thing a student wants is to look foolish. The brain prefers active learning and opportunities to test its powers by demonstrating skills and knowledge.

Where Would a Teacher Use Exhibitions and Presentations?
Any class as a culminating activity.

How Does a Teacher Use Exhibitions and Presentations?
The teacher informs the class that the culmination of a topic will be via an exhibition or presentation, preferably in a public venue, and establishes a firm date. Students will summarize what they learned via the exhibit or demonstration in lieu of an exam. Students either work individually or in teams to learn the material and then find creative ways

to present their work. The teacher becomes a valuable resource person to the individual students or teams.

For More Information
- www.essentialschools.org/cs/resources/view/ces_res/138
- www.essentialschools.org/cs/resources/view/ces_res/136

ENTREPRENEURSHIP

Entrepreneurship is students running a real business with a product or service for profit.

Examples of Entrepreneurship
- Students operate a school store as part of a class.
- Students start and operate a business making name badges.
- Students obtain contracts with small businesses to do graphic designing for ads and placards.
- Students operate an ethnic restaurant for staff or neighbors.

Why Use Entrepreneurship?
Students learn important skills and knowledge such as making a business plan, determining markup for a product, keeping books, salesmanship, and principles of economics. In the process, students use reading, writing, and arithmetic skills. Entrepreneurship programs generate enthusiasm and energy which means student brains are alive and receptive. Entrepreneurship brings reality to school lessons to deepen learning.

Where Would a Teacher Use Entrepreneurship?
At a simple level, any teacher might use a form of entrepreneurship by involving students in a fundraising activity such as selling cupcakes or a carwash. At a more serious level, social studies, math, industrial technology, and business education teachers could justify involving students in forming and operating a business.

How Does a Teacher Use Entrepreneurship?

While entrepreneurship units come up as a part of some programs, a more motivating process would involve discussions with students about operating a business, visits to other programs with entrepreneurship units, talks by community resource business people (don't forget diversity, here), brainstorming about possible products or services, outlining the steps necessary to begin a business, selecting teams for the various tasks, and implementing plans.

It is valuable to have frequent progress reports to discuss issues and problems so that classmates can learn from one another and offer suggestions. Equally important is debriefing and reflection as the businesses get underway and at the completion of the program.

For More Information

- ye.entreworld.org/
- www.edtecinc.com/edu_prods_nye.htm
- www.nfte.com/contact/

ORAL HISTORY

Oral history is having students tap into the knowledge and activities of people in the community through a process or recording information for future use.

Examples of Oral History

- Students write stories and take photographs as in the Foxfire magazine project.
- Students interview senior citizens about their lives.
- Students publish a book of poetry by local residents.

Why Use Oral History?

Important skills of interviewing, note-taking, summarizing information, meeting people, and having them feel at ease, photographing, writing, rewriting, and publishing are learned in the context of a real task of interest to students. Learning about real people and their lives is of high interest to students. Accordingly, oral histories pique student brains, and their brains become most receptive to learn, and the learning is deeper and more permanent.

Where Would a Teacher Use Oral History?

A teacher can use oral history to approach any subject, but perhaps it is most appropriate in English or social studies classes.

How Does a Teacher Use Oral History?

A teacher might start by asking students what questions they have about people and activities in the community. This can be followed up by asking, how students might best get answers to these questions.

The teacher can suggest that the direct approach of talking with people, recording their remarks accurately, and sharing their findings with a broader audience would be an exciting and effective learning experience. Many skills would be learned so that students could approach the task with confidence and professional competence.

For More Information

- www.foxfire.org/teachi.htm
- historymatters.gmu.edu/mse/oral
- library.ucsc.edu/reg-hist/ohprimer.html

Take a moment to assess the value of incorporating Oral History into your classroom.

1 2 3 4 5 6 7 8 9 10

VIDEOTAPING

Videotaping is using the power of media to capture an event for analysis or future presentation. Television equipment for the school or classroom has become far less expensive and is simpler to use and edit than in the past.

Examples of Videotaping

- A coach has students videotape other students in gymnastics to perfect moves.
- Students videotape elder citizens about their experiences in the armed services.
- Students videotape a skit to use as part of presentations over community video channels.

Why Use Videotaping?

Videotaping offers many experiences to exercise executive skills, such as decisions about who, what, when, and where to tape, editing for best effects, editing for content, the importance of accuracy and fairness, and perfecting skills and routines. Students greatly enjoy videotaping and it links to their own television viewing habits.

Where Would a Teacher Use Videotaping?

Any teacher sending students out to gather information can use videotaping as a way of capturing the information and using the intrinsic motivation students have about being given an important real assignment, using equipment, and viewing television. Videotaping can be used within the classroom and school to prepare presentations of information.

How Does a Teacher Use Videotaping?

A school needs to obtain basic equipment such as cameras with videotaping capability, handheld cameras, editing machines or editing software, and either videotape players or DVD players. Most schools have at least some of this equipment at present or it can be obtained for a fairly modest cost.

The manuals for the equipment provide helpful hints on how to use it. Some schools have contacted a local college for the use of one of their students in a video program to help students get started. Students also need instruction on the care of equipment. The teacher can be alert to situations that would benefit from videotaping.

Once students get started with videotaping, they will be eager to use their skills in videotaping and editing. Valuable skills including editing, writing a script, practicing a presentation, and sharing the results with an audience follow the actual interviewing and videotaping.

For More Information
- www.angelfire.com/ar2/videomanual1
- www.cecsep.usu.edu/resources/vcresources/vcvideotaping.htm

RETROSPECTIVE STRATEGY

Retrospective refers to studying an experience gained earlier by others to gain perspective about something new. Retrospective is a special type of reflection and by itself a powerful strategy.

Examples of Retrospective
- Graduates return to their former school to share their reflections with students or faculty.
- Students offer advice at the end of the year in individual letters to the students who will sit in their classroom seats.
- Dropouts explain to teachers why they left school.

Why Use Retrospective?
The unique first-person perspective gained from an experience that others are to repeat provides valuable information to the new candidate. Learners gain a sense of what it is like to "walk in another's shoes." The brain desires feedback in order to do its best and the experience of another is instructive. At such a stage, the brain is uniquely open to information. The person presenting the retrospective engages in a rigorous process of thinking, reflection, and organizing their thoughts.

Where Would a Teacher Use Retrospective?
Retrospectives can be used in any situation where learners encounter new situations and can profit from the experience of their predecessors.

How Does a Teacher Use Retrospective?

One teacher asked students to reflect on the school year and to put their thoughts in a letter of advice to the students who would occupy their desks in the coming year. Students were to suggest ways for the incoming student to be more successful in that class.

Inviting previous graduates to tell of their experiences in school provides valuable insights about how the program met students' needs and prepared them for the next stage of their lives. The same presentation to students will be particularly meaningful because of a role model effect.

www.infed.org/foundations/w-inf4.htm
www.unca.edu/et/br022102.html
www.studentsinservicetoamerica.org/tools_resources/docs/nwtoolkit.pdf

This chapter explains how thinking skills and learning strategies can be of value to teachers and students. Several anchor tools such as empirical scientific thinking, Bloom's Taxonomy, and Socratic Seminar were discussed.

This chapter shows how innovative methods such as Six Thinking Hats, Choice Boards, Cubing, role-playing, and more can help students improve their thinking skills. Students can also benefit from enriched experiences such as PLPs, learning exchanges, field trips, reading the newspaper, and participating in gallery walks.

Careful use of these strategies can sharpen students' thinking skills. The final outcome will be improved student confidence, comprehension, and achievement.

Webliography

- cnnstudentnews.cnn.com/fyi/
- coe.sdsu.edu/eet/Articles/jigsaw/index.htm
- dservices.aea7.k12.ia.us/framework/strategies/
- historymatters.gmu.edu/mse/oral
- http://homepage.tinet.ie/~denisdunne1/homework/k05.htm
- http://www.somers.k12.ny.us/intranet/reading/structuredideas.html
- library.ucsc.edu/reg-hist/ohprimer.html
- media3.iss.indiana.edu/htbin/wwform/www/?TEXT=R18279575-18283259-/www/documents/188/cat/wwi770.htm

- t4.jordan.k12.ut.us/Balanced_Literacy/Comprehension/cs_mental_imaging.htm
- web.odu.edu/webroot/orgs/Educ/Misc/MCTP.nsf/pages/eci795mctp_nalp
- www.accd.edu/sac/history/keller/ACCDitg/SSSQ3R.htm
- www.accessexcellence.org/AE/newatg/Haugen.sq3rplus
- www.afs.org
- www.angelfire.com/ar2/videomanual1
- www.bigpicture.org/MetPort96-7personalizedLearning.htm
- www.bsu.edu/teachers/services/ctr/javits/Instruction/Cubing.htm
- www.cecsep.usu.edu/resources/vcresources/vcvideotaping.htm
- www.concordhs.com/ateachsite/processing/gallerywalk.pdf
- www.edtecinc.com/edu_prods_nye.htm
- www.eduref.org/cgi-bin/printlessons.cgi/Virtual/Lessons/Language_Arts/Journalism/JNL0199.html
- www.essentialschools.org/cs/resources/view/ces_res/136
- www.essentialschools.org/cs/resources/view/ces_res/138
- www.eteamz.com/baseball/instruction/pitching/clinic.cfm/Mental%20Imaging/
- www.extension.iastate.edu/communities/tools/decisions/nominal.html
- www.foxfire.org/teachi.htm
- www.gamos.demon.co.uk/sustainable/hatpap.htm
- www.graphic.org/links.html
- www.gsn.org/project/fieldtrips
- www.infed.org/foundations/w-inf4.htm
- www.mcps.k12.md.us/departments/eii/diffexemplaryex.html#Cubing
- www.msue.msu.edu/msue/imp/modii/iii00005.html
- www.naturalmaths.com.au/Settings/six_hats.htm
- www.ncrel.org/sdrs/areas/issues/students/learning/lr1kwlh.htm
- www.ncrel.org/sdrs/areas/issues/students/learning/lr2refer.htm
- www.ncrel.org/sdrs/areas/issues/students/learning/lr2refer.htm
- www.ncrel.org/sdrs/areas/rpl_esys/collab.htm
- www.ncwiseowl.org/webquest/spider/Spider%20WebQuest%20KWLH%20Handout.html
- www.newhorizons.org/strategies/democratic/kennedy.htm
- www.nfte.com/contact/
- www.nhs.us/pdf/nslc04_adultstaffapp.doc
- www.nwse.com

- www.oznet.ksu.edu/LEADS/FACT%20Sheets/fact2.pdf
- www.post1.com/home/garytsu/ITLessonProcess.htm
- www.principals.org/pdf/nlc_2004brochure.pdf
- www.servicelearning.org/
- www.socraticseminars.com/whatare.htm
- www.stenhouse.com/pdfs/8134fm.pdf
- www.studentsinservicetoamerica.org/tools_resources/docs/nwtoolkit.pdf
- www.studyguide.org/socratic_seminar.htm
- www.suelebeau.com/nie.htm
- www.teach-nology.com/web_tools/graphic_org/
- www.u.arizona.edu/ic/wrightr/other/sq3r.html
- www.unca.edu/et/br022102.html
- www.yfu-usa.org
- ye.entreworld.org/

NOTES

1. Guskey, Thomas R. Lessons of mastery learning! *Educational Leadership*, 68 (2), 2010. p. 52–57.
2. Given, Barbara. Theaters of the mind. *Educational Leadership*, 58 (3), 2000. p. 72–75.
3. Dunston, P.J. A critique of graphic organizer research. *Reading Research and Instruction*, 31 (2), 1992. p. 57–65.
4. Jennings, Wayne, and Joan Caulfield. *Bridging the Learning/Assessment Gap: Showcase Teaching*. Lanham, MD: Scarecrow Education, 2005. p. 63.

Chapter 2

Leveraging the Power of Technology

TECHNOLOGY

Essential Question: *How can leveraging the power of technology improve teaching and learning?*

Most of us can't imagine navigating our tasks and lives without the aid of technology and its ability to relieve us of tedious tasks. Youth have grown up with technology and think nothing of exploring its useful and exciting applications. Technology has been the long sought-after means for increasing learning. Each development with technology became the hoped-for Holy Grail of education.

Many thought radios and then television offered remarkable ways to augment instruction, or by some advocates, increase school staff differentiation, thereby reallocating resources. Radio and television technologies did not have much of an effect, though television has survived, barely.

Most school or district storerooms have boxes of long-playing records and tapes, unknown or ignored by teachers still in favor of textbooks with their well-organized and meticulously prepared lessons.

Too often in the past, teachers were busy delivering content and did not make time for using technology—it was one more task to manage and integrate into lessons. Teachers had subjects to teach, and curriculum manuals tightly orchestrated those.

Only simple overhead projectors survived for decades with their ease of use to amplify information and augment the trustworthy chalkboard.

Computer-controlled PowerPoint-type programs replaced overhead projectors and were the primary use of technology in recent years.

In this age, students have access to information anytime, anywhere, with or without teachers. Cell phone technology presents an entry to the world's information with a few clicks of a thumb. Teachers saddled with covering school subjects abandoned their instructional dreams of becoming exciting teachers confronted with ubiquitous standardized tests.

Tests and predetermined curricula cannot or do not provide opportunities for students to follow interests. Only the most persistent and time-efficient teachers manage to integrate technology with mastery of content.

Now people dictate words into a microphone, and they magically appear on the monitor. Imagine the day when a six-year-old tells a story about his or her family, and the words appear immediately on the computer. Could that revolutionize the teaching of reading or speed its development? If so, this would be an amazing use of technology.

Some of the recent software (many suggested by Amy Meuers, CEO of the National Council for Youth Leadership): WeVideo, Easely, Anchor, Inspiration, Animate-it, Picktochart, Canva, Powtoon, and Emaze (create videos, newsletters, and presentations); Flipgrid (discussions); Padlets (media); Vibe, Jamboard (brainstorming and group processing of ideas), and Zoho Writer, LibreOffice, Google Docs, Flipbook, yWriter, Evernote, Novelize, Ulysses, Scrivener, FastPencil, Word (book writing), are very useful, among other software options.

We suggest having students explore these (such as one piece of software for a team of two students) and make presentations to alert teachers and students to the possibilities of using the new technologies.

New programs appear with remarkable features that may replace segments of the current curriculum. Futurists say, with a nod to their lack of grammar, "You ain't seen nothin yet!" Artificial intelligence may make, augment, and replace much of today's technological wonders.

Teachers can access an astonishing array of resources such as National Geographic, Nova, PBS, and high-quality sites on history, arts, culture, people, literature, science, and geography. During sharing sessions, other teachers will suggest new resources they have uncovered.

A topic like the transcontinental railroad triggers pictures using the images feature of Google. Subsets of the transcontinental railroad topic could enrich understanding and offer follow-on activities for students.

Also, consider how diverse subjects such as wildlife, magic, architecture, dogs, crocheting help students build on personal interest areas. The interest hardly matters when it comes to resources to satisfy pursuits.

As seen in figures 2.1 and 2.2, inexpensive computers (Chromebooks with free software, for example) and cheap internet access in schools make the recent goal of 1-1 computer to student ratio feasible. Students catch on to new technologies quickly and, if asked, are happy to help their teachers gain expertise.

Ideally, every teacher and every student has a computer. The lower costs of computers and printers make this a reality. Consider how such diverse subjects as wildlife, ESP, architecture, dog training, and tides extend personal interests.

Today's technology encompasses a wide spectrum of tools: internet, computers, word processing, student-made videos, satellite receivers, electronic classrooms, whiteboards, radio stations, television studios, remote databases, cloud storage, desktop publishing, scanners, graphics, clip art, response systems, optical character recognition (OCR), and more.

Students catch on to new technologies quickly and, if asked, are happy to help their teachers gain expertise. Ideally, every teacher and

Figure 2.1 Livy Niermann and Jack Niermann. *Source:* Photography by Tom Niermann.

every student would have a computer. The substantially lower costs of computers and printers make that a reality.

With the information resources of the twenty-first century, students and lifelong learning adults can take advantage anytime in the future of appropriately needed learning. The world's stock of information doesn't have to be implanted by age eighteen. If used to its potential, technology is the wild card for learning. Teachers using technology can more effectively enrich and convey content.

Many people use Google or other search engines to find information. Beyond a simple search, researchers use Google Scholar and Talk to Books for advanced information. The latter responds to a normal sentence type question and searches 100,000 books in less than one second to bring up answers and ideas. Try it; they have sample questions for a test.

Entire libraries are being digitized for rapid access and making available precious or rare information. With technological advances, students will learn more. We might ask more of what? Hopefully, more of what the school's mission expects.

Khan Academy and its like, YouTube and its similar platforms, Wikipedia, TED Talks, and worldwide courses inform and provide tools to increase many-fold enjoyable, timely learning. We can't imagine the technologies of tomorrow that students will encounter during their lifetimes. Luddite personalities don't fit the times nor prepare students for their post-school lives.

About three decades ago, response systems came on the scene and they are sill in use, mostly at the college level and business level. Response systems provide instant feedback to an instructor on the extent of learning by students. Cables connected student "clickers" to the teacher counsel—a bothersome rats-nest of wires. Now, wireless systems replace cords. Clickers enable the teacher to gauge learning.

With clickers in the hands of each student responding to teacher questions, they choose one of the answers. Teachers can use response systems beyond facts and concepts by trolling for opinions or reactions to, for example, a short passage, an election, or a controversial topic. Unfortunately, as attractive as this technology is, the expense is high to equip all or many classrooms. Nonetheless, a school could establish one area with response technology.

The need to answer kept students attending. The teacher obtains rapid feedback from the class. If half of the class gave the wrong answer, the teacher could reteach the material. Some teachers turned the screen toward the students so the class could see the distribution of answers. Clickers gave students a sense of anonymity, yet, teachers immediately knew who had responded.

Response systems were not limited to appraising facts and concepts. Innovative teachers trolled for opinions or reactions to, for example, a short passage. Unfortunately, attractive as this technology was, the expense was high to equip all or many classrooms.

Some clever person found a way to duplicate clicker technology inexpensively. After a teacher question, students held up a sheet of paper marked on both sides, with a different symbol for the four areas of the paper (turned upright or down, and both sides).

The symbols yielded four choices. The teacher scanned the raised sheets and could swiftly judge the accuracy of student responses. This simple response system hasn't caught on, although anyone could profitably use it in any classroom setting.

A valuable use of telephone technology occurred when a speakerphone enabled teachers and students to interview someone remotely. The interviewee might be a person reluctant to allocate travel and interviewing time but willing to talk by phone.

This simple technology never took root to any significant degree, mainly because teachers did not have telephones in their classroom. Cell phone technology with an inexpensive speaker solves the lack of classroom landline telephones.

Marc Prensky referred to students as digital natives because students pick up technology as though built into their psyche. He described most adults, especially older adults, as digital immigrants struggling to understand how to use software and to understand youth culture and language.

Adult comfort has changed as more use their cell phones beyond calling someone. Adults, even grandparents, take and send pictures, make to-do lists, and look up information. Almost every adult has had the experience of seeing another person use their cell phone in a novel way, and says, "Wow, I didn't know you could do that." Cell phones are computers and capable of many functions. Cell phones have bridged the technology stalemate for teachers.

Students have invented a youth language of abbreviations, grammar, and novel spellings like lol (laughing out loud), pos for parent over shoulder (and thus be careful what you say). Would students' conventional spelling, writing, and reading improve based on the hundreds of instant messages students write, send, and read? We don't know.

Students communicate thoughts and ideas, even socially unacceptable ones. Many contain erroneous information that are, unfortunately, broadcast to a network of possibly thousands or more.

A healthier use of cell phone messaging emerged with students' interest in global warming and environmental safety. Students communicated that problem to millions of others instantaneously. It led to student protest marches and may sway decision-makers action. Not a bad result! And, a valuable opportunity for teaching appropriate actions and their consequences.

The use of cell phones by students is nearly ubiquitous (and annoying to people nearby) even with students from low-income neighborhoods. Once again, expectations ran high that cell phone technologies would redesign K-12 education. For some teachers, allowing students to use their cell phones to look up information is welcomed in the classroom. This technique sometimes can create a sense of excitement over who can find the most relevant information first.

Experts estimate that students use cell phones for instant messaging hundreds of times a day. Every year, new social technologies appear, and students adapt and adopt faster than adults. The remedy: Have students teach teachers how to design applications of technology into subjects.

Students can now forward homework to their teacher, sometimes a few seconds before a deadline. Speed and less paper yield advantages. Even electronic versions of teacher grade books provide a quicker tallying of absences, calculating test score averages, and creating printouts.

Khan Academy and others provide instruction on an immense variety of skills and knowledge, often self-paced with a built-in record-keeping system for teachers. Khan Academy initially began for K-12 mathematics but now provides lessons for other school subjects. This amazing development is always carefully touted as augmenting teacher instruction rather than teacher replacement.

YouTube and similar websites provide information on almost any subject. For example, a friend wondered how they made terrazzo floors; another looked up American Indian pow wows; one repaired a washing machine himself for far less cost by referencing an online manual; others learned about holidays, how to perform a magic trick, bird migration routes, and an endless quantity of video topics.

Search a question and an answer arrives in a millisecond—an incredible difference from the days of looking up something in an encyclopedia across the room on a bookshelf and thumbing the pages.

Florida Virtual School (FLVS) founded in 1997, as the first statewide K-12 internet-based public high school in the United States, grew rapidly. The Florida legislature funded development of all subjects from kindergarten to high-school graduation. It enrolled students initially from Florida and later from throughout the United States and the world.

Several commercial vendors sell online curricula that students master from home or community sites such as a library. Some online schools provide computers and pay internet fees: however, the number of schools who still extend such benefits are Increasing.

In one instance, a state indicted an online school for not covering all levels of mathematics. The suit dragged on in the courts, and ultimately, the school won by showing its availability of the courses under question. The thoroughness of learning raised doubts, and questioned the honesty of students without supervision of teachers.

Technology made possible massive open online courses with an enrollment, sometimes of thousands, of students from distant places. Some students dropped out for lack of interest or keeping up with assignments.

Administrators find online learning less expensive despite questions about its effectiveness (note: typical classroom coursework has problems of its own). Some innovative online instructors develop greater student interaction with a question by the instructor or, better, by a student. When students answer one after the other, peer to peer interaction increases, thereby enhancing understanding. Misconceptions melt, and brilliant new ideas may emerge.

Internet technology is degrees of scale ahead of older technologies and has the potential of generating greater student interest. Can we call the new technologies a paradigm change, or instructional reform, revolution, or transformation? Enormous adult factual knowledge increases with technology in every scope of life, in presidential elections, and global conflicts. Most older people knew nothing about countries and cultures of the Near East. Now many do.

This book about optimizing learning proposes a greater degree of student-*centered* learning, perhaps even student-*directed* learning.

In both instances, textbook and lectures, mostly antithetical to brain-compatible learning, can be reduced or eliminated for greater student engagement as we suggest.

Can we give up the notion that we have to learn every subject's content by age eighteen? Can we accept that school has a major purpose, that of advancing lifelong learning? Can we trust that much of school instruction can be postponed until needed, if ever? Most of us relearned important concepts as adults when we sought more information on a topic (e.g., in appraising the positions of candidates for election).

Technology permits just-in-time learning, even changing one's entire career. Technology requires schools to teach the use of technology and its limitations. For example, internet information may not be accurate or up-to-date. Fraudulent information can be found, such as the one website stating that the Holocaust never occurred. Its authenticity seems correct because the information is promoted not by the University but a professor, as indicated by internet grammar (~).

The Flat Earth Society has a website promoting their position with a newsletter, library of books, and testimonials, thus "proving" their views. Like advertisements, websites present valuable classroom lessons for critical thinking skills.

With online learning of various types, we face not a gradual change of schooling but rather radical change.

With technological approaches, we create a new paradigm on schooling.

For example, a student-directed approach puts learning in the hands of students rather than determined solely by the teacher, textbook, state or district curricula, and standardized tests. Some argue that these several factors handcuff teachers; others, traditionalists say the same factors bring clarity to the curriculum.

The newer technologies may change schooling in a way that the older technologies did not. Barriers of covering subjects left little time for teachers to study how to integrate the various technologies as they arose. Few teacher preparation programs touch on the use of technology.

Teachers' prior experiences as students reinforced the paradigm of rows of desks with the teacher in front. Every TV and movie strengthens this image. At present, in contrast with former times, conventional educational practice will change or be replaced. Maintaining jobs can be a powerful incentive for change.

Technology may help with the problems of dropouts and disengagement. Studies show disengagement rates of about 50 percent of highschool students. Technology, especially with the advent of artificial intelligence (AI), may personalize instruction for academic level, interest level, and learning style.

Technology will adjust lessons automatically. This technology isn't as far-fetched as it seems. Automated testing does this to a degree presently. But as the saying goes, "you ain't seen anything yet."

Students may maintain electronic portfolios with information gleaned from the internet and other sources, personal notes, graphics, and photographs. These may constitute a history of school work not limited by a sheaf of unchanging paper, and not in a physical location, but cloud-based storage. This may seem far-fetched to us, but actually, it's not far from word processing, and saving a document, with student-created graphics.

Student-directed learning addresses not only content but also social and emotional growth. Giving students greater opportunities for expression and exploring personal interests with personal creation of products enhance self-regarding attitudes. It may display to the teacher negative thinking in a manner invisible with canned textbook lessons.

Some years ago, futurists advanced, "Principal on a chip." By that, they meant major categories of a principal's professional life activities, each subdivided into detailed issues. Each of these would contain remedies.

For example, a student sent to the office for some transgression would have details entered for the type of transgression, age, previous incidents, and the prior remedies used. Such information would be entered via voice much as medical doctors enter information into patient records, now. A computer would spit out a remedy. Some might argue the physical principal could handle this work quickly and more effectively. Still, who knows what future AI may bring?

With a little thought, we recognize that even old technologies such as movies and television programs have changed our lives immensely (e.g., racial and gender equity). There is more to be done on these, but what has happened was thought nearly impossible and far-off in the future for its enactment. The changes were not from educational leadership but court decisions.

One problem with technology involves enthusiasts who wish to apply a technological remedy to everything, thus promoting technology for

Figure 2.2 Mia Matthews-Beaven. *Source:* Photography by Doug Hesse. Image rights—STA.

technology's sake. We don't know the far reaches of technology, but each new device or program needs a rational appraisal.

A few suggestions for incorporating technology into teaching:

- Use technology by expanding your interest and skills of word processing. For example, use a search engine (fancy term for a way to find information) like Google, Google Scholar, Safari, and Talk to Books to find ideas for any topic.
- Ask students to explain their knowledge of technology (such as social media) and why they use it. The pluses and minuses could be a discussion or assigned writing—some of the most provocative read to the class for comments. The students will give examples of pros and cons. You will learn what attracts kids to spending so much time with social media.
- Ask kids how they might use their cell phones to find information about the topic. For example, they might ask an authority if they would accept an interview. Students will learn that authorities have gatekeepers that prevent people from wasting the time of their bosses.
- They will learn a way of handling such query and an interview. They should learn in advance the authorities' position and carefully explain

their interest to the gatekeeper; write a carefully worded question or submit an essay for the authorities thoughts; ask for an opportunity for a face-to-face interview; learn that persistence often works; learn that failure will occur. If successful, prepare students on how to conduct an effective dialogue.
- Have students prepare a graphic or cartoon about a current topic. Look up other cartoons for their take on the subject. This gives opportunities for students to explain to their peers how graphics communicate concepts.
- Use tutorials to learn a useful technology tool. Most technology software has tutorials.

None of these ideas will work unless a teacher welcomes new practices and devotes time to what may not initially appear a useful source of information.

While there is no perfect formula in terms of the best types of technology to use in the classroom, the good news is that there are various, new options for consideration. Each classroom teacher will need to discover the best tools to help students become digital natives.

Kibben suggests that students not only want to use technology but also have greater agency in creating and cocreating technology.[1] In some technology, options can make educational tasks more dynamic and playful. Anytime students are able to engage with their learning in a fun way, chances are that they will have a sustained focus on their work.

Technology lends itself to providing an immersive, interactive experience, and it enables students to seamlessly and efficiently collaborate with each other in an instant.

McKissack Public School in Nashville, Tennessee, for example, is a model school for incorporating technology as part of project-based learning where Promethean interactive whiteboards and mobile technology carts that have integrated Dell Latitude laptops facilitate STEAM (science, technology, engineering, art, and mathematics) collaborative learning projects.[2]

There is no denying that technology is here to stay. By no means does this chapter discuss all of the technological options for classroom use, as there are a plethora of options available. The following represents a list of a few top technology considerations for classroom teachers to explore.

1. Google Drive

Google Drive is an impressive digital platform that allows users to create, search, and store files. It allows users to access files from any device. Google Drive has many great features including Google Docs that functions as a word processor to edit documents. Multiple users can work together in real-time on Google Documents. There are other Google add-ons that include the following:

- **Google Sheets**: allows users to create spreadsheets.
- **Google Slides**: allows users to create slide presentations that are easy to edit online or offline.
- **Google Maps**: allows users to see satellite imagery and engage in real-time route planning.

Google also allows users to connect to its Google Workspace Marketplace for more platforms that work with Google (e.g., platforms such as Lucid Press, Lucid Charts, just to name a few).

For more information about Google Drive visit:

google.com/intl/en_zm/drive/

Take a moment to assess the value of incorporating Google Drive into your classroom

1   2   3   4   5   6   7   8   9   10

2. Microsoft Teams

Microsoft Teams is a platform that allows users to engage in real-time chatting and/or videoconferencing. Users will receive individual workspace for files and landing space for documents. The main benefits of Teams are that it enhances communication and collaboration capabilities in the following ways:

- Users can communicate with each other one-to-one or in groups.
- Subcategories can be designed to allow for special assignment groups and breakout rooms.

- Teachers can live-stream and record their classes and meetings using built-in Teams video technology.
- Users can also participate in live streaming video discussions through the integrated Flipgrid video tool. This tool helps students respond to their teachers and peers in open platform discussions.

For more information about Microsoft Teams visit:

https://www.microsoft.com/en-us/microsoft-365/microsoft-teams/group-chat-software

Take a moment to assess the value of incorporating Microsoft Teams into your classroom

    1   2   3   4   5   6   7   8   9   10

3. OneNote/OneNote Class Notebook

Microsoft Teams also features OneNote Class digital notebooks that can allow teachers to manage assignments, transfer files, and provide comments to their students. Some of the benefits of OneNote Notebooks are:

- The digital notebooks allow for easy access and organization.
- Notebooks can also be easily shared with other users for collaboration.
- OneNote Class Notebooks automatically save notes that are entered in the OneDrive cloud for easy retrieval.

For more information about OneNote Class Notebooks visit:

https://www.onenote.com/classnotebook

Take a moment to assess the value of incorporating OneNote Class Notebooks into your classroom.

    1   2   3   4   5   6   7   8   9   10

4. Flipgrid

Flipgrid is a video discussion platform available from Microsoft. Teachers are able to pose a question to their students and allow them to respond back in video form. The platform is great for use within the physical classroom or in a virtual classroom format.

For more information about Flipgrid visit: https://flipgrid.com

Take a moment to assess the value of incorporating Flipgrid into your classroom.

      1   2   3   4   5   6   7   8   9   10

5. Dugga

Dugga is an integrated platform available from Microsoft that allows teachers to create a variety of assessments and assignments via text, audio, or video. The results can then be easily graded and sent back to students in a timely fashion.

For more information about Dugga visit: https: dugga.com

Take a moment to assess the value of incorporating Dugga into your classroom.

      1   2   3   4   5   6   7   8   9   10

6. EdPuzzle

EdPuzzle is a classroom video tool that teachers can use to flip their classroom learning structure. Students are able to view the videos at their own pace and interact with the information for individualized learning.

The tool allows students to auto-pause the video to ask questions, and these questions can be sent to the teacher. Teachers can add audio comments to any video including videos imported from YouTube to enhance the instruction.

For more information about EdPuzzle visit: https://edpuzzle.com/

Take a moment to assess the value of incorporating EdPuzzle into your classroom.

1   2   3   4   5   6   7   8   9   10

7. Movavi

Movavi is a video editing software that teachers can use to enhance their videos with special effects and exciting animations.

For more information about Movai visit:

https://www.movavi.com/suite-unlimited/?asrc=main_menu#main

Take a moment to assess the value of incorporating Movai into your classroom.

1   2   3   4   5   6   7   8   9   10

8. iPad (and related Apps)

An iPad is a portable, flat tablet made by Apple Inc. that can perform all of the functions that a computer can do such as browsing the web, watching videos, and providing word processing functions. Various tablet sizes are available, and many built-in apps are available that can be very helpful to teachers and exciting for students to use. Some of the most popular apps that can be downloaded into the iPad include:

- **Notability**: Notability allows for word processing on the iPad and users can make documents with texts, images, or sound.
- **Book Creator**: Book Creator is a book-making tool where users can design their own books and journals with colorful illustrations and other creative content.
- **iMovie**: iMovie allows users to create exciting film presentations about their learning.
- **Explain Everything**: Explain Everything is a whiteboard tool that allows users to annotate, narrate, and import/export creations. Users can also create slides and manipulate photos and documents from the iPad.
- **Pages**: Pages allows for Word Processing on the iPad where users can design publications from templates or a blank document.

- **Socrative**: Teachers can create quizzes that are automatically graded by the app.
- **Seesaw App**: Seesaw is a classroom app that allows users to create digital portfolios of their classroom learning.
- **Kahoot App**: Kahoot is a game-based application that allows teachers to create multiple-choice quizzes or trivia questions for classroom use.

To learn more about the iPad visit: https://www.apple.com/ipad/

Take a moment to assess the value of incorporating the iPad and the aforementioned apps into your classroom.

1 2 3 4 5 6 7 8 9 10

This chapter outlines why technology is an important tool to enhance student learning. Technology provides interactive, heads-on experiences that can increase connectivity between students and their classroom community members.

There are a range of fun, technological applications that teachers and students can choose from. Some of the technologies include computers, iPad, and an array of applications including Google Docs, Padlets, Flipbook, Microsoft Teams, Dugga, EdPuzzle, and more. Technology improves classroom learning because it makes organization of information a seamless experience.

Teachers have an obligation to help students become competent, digital users of technology, in other words digital natives. To be successful in the twenty-first century, they must know how to effectively use and explore as many technological resources as possible.

NOTES

1. McKibben, Sarah. *Educational Leadership* 76 (5), February 2019. p. 51.
2. Hayes, Heather. Bringing lessons to life. *EdTEch*, 2019. p. 23.

WEBLIOGRAPHY

google.com/intl/en_zm/drive/
https: dugga.com
https://edpuzzle.com/
https://flipgrid.com
https://www.apple.com/ipad/
https://www.microsoft.com/en-us/microsoft-365/microsoft-teams/group-chat-software
https://www.movavi.com/suite-unlimited/?asrc=main_menu#main
https://www.onenote.com/classnotebook

Chapter 3

Harnessing the Power of Teaming

TEAMING

Essential Question: *How can harnessing the power of team learning improve student achievement?*

Teachers face an important challenge: How can they ensure deep and substantive learning for each individual student when their classroom rosters are full of multiple pupils with diverse needs? This question is certainly a daunting one, as teachers are also managing routine clerical duties, overseeing behavior management of students, and a host of other demanding, ancillary responsibilities. Yet, there are sound and helpful teaming strategies if effectively implemented can make a world of difference.

The way to navigate the dilemma is to consider frameworks for team learning. This chapter explores how cooperative team learning frameworks alleviate some of the pressures teachers face in their attempts to teach all students.

DEFINING TEAMING

Team learning also known as cooperative learning in the traditional sense is a teaching strategy that provides students with the opportunity for academic and social learning. It has become increasingly difficult because of the COVID-19 pandemic to physically group students together as teachers customarily did in the past. Nonetheless, with creative thinking and technological advances, team learning should remain a staple teaching strategy in every instructor's toolkit.

Rather than implementing team learning in occasional spurts, every teacher should regard team learning as an essential anchor, the focal linchpin that when coupled with other strategies can create a successful classroom culture.

Teachers should implement team learning opportunities in a systematic fashion in order to foster a sense of routine acceptance and classroom comfort. When integrating team learning, teachers should strive for multiple ways of facilitating the technique.

The best cooperative team learning methods will require a careful gauge and awareness of the classroom population of learners. Development of optimal techniques best suited for each teacher's students is crucial. Such techniques, then, will facilitate the continuing achievements of the teacher's students.

Once a teacher has formulated a strategic amount of team learning options, the techniques can be sharpened and improved each day. Teachers will find it helpful to review and hone their team learning methods to ensure rigor and continuing vivacity in the classroom environment.

Some Basic Benefits of Team Learning:

- Provides an opportunity for shared cognitive information and opinions between students.
- Creates greater accountability and motivation for learning.
- Facilitates a user-friendly way to obtain formative assessments.
- Increases positive relationships both in and out of the classroom.

CREATING TEAM CULTURE

Teachers around the world have successfully demonstrated the effectiveness of grouping students together for team learning. When students are able to work together meaningfully and hold each other individually accountable, the classroom teacher can be alleviated from the responsibility of orchestrating every single minute of classroom conversation. Thoughtful, structured, and effective organization will prevent the classroom environment from becoming disorderly.

As shown in figures 3.1 and 3.2, no matter the age of the learners, the reality is that they look forward to time with each other away from their teacher's concentrated gaze. Early childhood research confirms that even though students may find their teachers likeable and very pleasant to learn from and be around, as they age and ascend through the grades they have a preference for spending more time with their classmate peers.[1]

The teacher is pivotal in establishing classroom norms to create a productive team learning culture. The teacher will need to help students understand how to listen to each other as they work on shared learning project goals. Students really benefit when they can engage with each other and hear different perspectives regarding their learning task.

Editor in Chief at the Buck Institute for Education, John Larmer makes clear that, "Teachers can support students' teamwork in many ways: constructing a list of norms or a rubric with students; having students write contracts for how they will work together."[2]

The necessity of establishing clear structures to facilitate successful team learning cannot be emphasized enough. Clear structures or norms represent agreements of team members to facilitate the work to be accomplished. Team norms might be as simple as allowing one team member to speak at a time, maintaining eye contact when a group member is speaking, or agreeing not to interrupt each other when someone is speaking, and so on.

The specific norm agreements will vary depending upon the age and abilities of the students involved. When students have clear guidelines about how to work together in their team learning groups, they will have greater success in learning. Should students encounter any difficulties in their team configurations, the classroom teacher will need to intervene to get students back on track.

A necessary component of facilitating successful teaming is teacher involvement. Some teachers mistakenly think that students can be grouped together without any teacher interaction needed. Teachers must stand nearby at all times in close proximity, in order to help their students reach learning goals and task completion.

Figure 3.1 Tyler Carlson. *Source:* Photography by Stephanie Carlson.

STRUCTURING TEAMS

There are a number of considerations to keep in mind when structuring teams of students together. The teacher is responsible for creating productive team structures that will benefit each student member's success. Before putting students together in teams, the teacher must have a sense of each student capability and personality. It is important to assemble a diverse group of thinkers together so that students can draw from each other's strengths.

There are definite benefits of stronger ability students working with those whose skills are not as sharp. The teacher should emphasize the importance of partnership so that each student recognizes how they play a critical role in helping the team's success. To prevent any team member from dominating the discussion or taking over team's activities, it is vital for the teacher to remind students of their classroom team norms.

SUSTAINING TEAM LEARNING MOMENTUM

A variety of team learning tasks are important for sustaining students' attention for short-term learning and future learning. Student's interest will be more effective when they have the opportunity to engage in dialogue about their learning.

The teacher must ensure that all students within the teams understand their expected roles during the team learning process. Should students not take their learning or roles seriously, the teacher's responsibility is to insist on accountability.

An important aspect of sustaining team learning momentum is continuous feedback and assessment.

Teachers can use a variety of methods to assess students individually or collectively, depending on the objectives to be measured. A teacher can learn a great deal about each student's understanding by carefully looking at every student's individual effort. Through careful observation, a teacher will be able to see if any of the students have struggles or deficits in their learning. Performance assessments that require student team members to demonstrate their critical or creative thinking skills are very helpful.

Research on assessment shows that teachers can have students engage in varied, performance-based cooperative speaking and project learning activities and use rating scales to assess individual students' achievements.[3] While these diverse exercises may vary in intensity, they all involve teaming; yet, the performance-based activities facilitate individual learning.

Several team activities are fun, necessary, and helpful to keep students engaged. Teachers can consider some of the following team strategies for their students.

TEAM ACTIVITIES

Research Teaming

A shared research project where students can collaborate on a common topic is an excellent way to facilitate learning. When students can approach their contributions to team projects as seriously as advisers in the White House's Situation Room do, the activity can lead to terrific cooperative learning. This activity is best suited for middle and high-school students.

How to Establish a Research Team?

- Assign specific topics of study to groups of four to five students. For example, perhaps the topics could be about animals, historical figures, scientists, the continents, and so on.
- Arrange the students in circle format.
- Give students note cards with specific directions outlining their aspect to research.
- Provide students with designated time to perform their research work.
- Gather students back as a group to dialogue about their findings.
- The students can proceed to document their research and compile a collaborative report.
- Each group will reassemble as a collective class to share their findings.

Take a moment to assess the value of incorporating Research Teaming into your classroom.

    1   2   3   4   5   6   7   8   9   10

Group-Think Teaming

Group-think is a cooperative way for students to brainstorm and study curricular issues. It is essentially a tabletop exercise that allows for students to combine their critical thinking skills to contemplate a challenging question. This activity is suitable for all ages.

How to Facilitate Group-Think Teaming?

- The teacher should pose a challenging, grade-appropriate question related to math, science, language arts, social studies, music, art, and so on. For example, the teacher might ask, what rare animals are near extinction?
- Students are placed in small groups to discuss the question.
- A specific time allotment should be announced to tackle the problem.
- The group can designate one recorder to jot down each person's ideas.
- Each group member must participate in thinking and sharing ideas about the problem.

- The teacher can decide if the students must work from memory or use research in their findings.
- The group-think teamwork will cease when the teacher calls time.
- The class should reconvene and share their group-think findings.

Take a moment to assess the value of incorporating Group-Think Teaming into your classroom.

    1   2   3   4   5   6   7   8   9   10

Chart Matrix Teaming

Generative thinking using charts is an excellent way for students to compile their perspectives on a variety of topics. When students can gather together in small teams and visually chart their ideas using graphic circles, squares, or triangles in a chart form, it is an excellent way to organize information for team learning. Chart Matrix Teaming is suitable for all ages.

How to Facilitate Chart Matrix Teaming?

- Allow students to create their own charts or provide them with print copies of a chart matrix structure.
- The students should work together to categorize their ideas to showcase common or different characteristics.
- Each team member should contribute ideas for the chart.
- The class should reconvene and share their findings with the whole class.

Take a moment to assess the value of incorporating Chart Matrix Teaming into your classroom.

    1   2   3   4   5   6   7   8   9   10

Concentric Circles Teaming

Concentric circles teaming is a fun way for two-student groups to work together. Groups will come together to think about new information or review prior students. This strategy is designed to energize students of all ages by allowing a bit of movement. It is a short-term activity that should be used for no more than fifteen minutes.

How to Facilitate Concentric Circles Teaming?

- Invite pairs of students to stand. Aim to assemble eight to ten students per group.
- Students should form an inner circle and a surrounding outer circle to pair a corresponding partner around the perimeter of each inner circle student.
- Once the circle configurations are in place, the inner circle students should turn around to face their outer circle student partner.
- The teacher should give questions to the outside circle students on note cards, paper, or via a technology device.
- The outside circle students should begin posing questions to their partners. A sample question might be, "Why was Benjamin the antagonist in our classroom reading?"
- The outside partner listens carefully for the correct answer and fills in any gaps of missing information.
- An additional question is posed before the inside circle clockwise movement starts.
- The inside circle moves two steps inside the circle (two people over) to face a different outside partner.
- The new outside partner poses a new question to his/her peer.
- The process can then reverse by flipping the process so that the inside circle group has an opportunity to question the exterior circle peers.

Take a moment to assess the value of incorporating Concentric Circles Teaming into your classroom.

      1   2   3   4   5   6   7   8   9   10

Literature Teaming

Literature Teaming is a way for students to come together to discuss and understand literary works, history readings, science, and more. This strategy is suitable for all grade levels.

The goal is for students to engage with each other about something they will read or have read. Literature Teaming heightens reading interest and allows students to share their ideas with each other. The technique helps spark students' critical and creative thinking skills. The time for this activity will vary depending on the length of the chosen reading material.

How to Facilitate Literature Teaming?
- The teacher assembles students into working team groups.
- The teacher provides the focal reading that can either be read in advance or the group can engage in the reading in real-time.
- After reading the material, the students should summarize the information together and/or respond to specific teacher-designed questions.
- To extend the learning further, the teacher can invite students to change the plot and create an alternate ending to the reading material.
- As an artistic exercise, the group can work together to illustrate scenes of their reading.
- Following completion of the team work, each group can then share out their responses and creations.

Take a moment to assess the value of incorporating Literature Teaming into your classroom.

1   2   3   4   5   6   7   8   9   10

Game Teaming

Students are competitive by nature, so a teacher can easily tap into their love of competing to review classroom learning. Game teaming allows students to huddle and think together in family style groups, or line up and tag their next partners in line to solve a challenge. Team members have the opportunity to think together and challenge one another in a fun way. Game teaming is suitable for all ages.

A game is an activity involving a playful situation in which students compete (sometimes cooperate) in order to win. Games are simulations that students respond to with excitement and energy.

Examples of Games:
- Students play Jeopardy about historical information.
- Student teams compete for best scores on informal exams in science.
- Student expert panel responds to questions from the class in culture studies.

Why Use Games?

Students enjoy games because they bring amusement and fun into drab, humdrum school lives. During games, students' minds are alive and alert, thus more learning of various kinds occurs. Students receive praise and encouragement from fellow team members, always a valuable practice.

Where Would a Teacher Use Games?

Any class, any subject to spark interest and enthusiasm.

How Does a Teacher Use Games?

Students are pretty good at making up games so a teacher might ask if there is any way to make a game out of learning the material. Teachers can use popular television programs as a format for games. Teachers can use the material scheduled for review or examination as game content and an alternative process of preparing for an exam.

How to Facilitate Sample Game Teaming?

- The teacher divides the students into cooperative teams. At least two teams are needed.
- The teams are designated as Team A or Team B, or the groups can be allowed to think of their own names.
- The teacher should have desired questions ready to pose to the groups.
- A designated student from Team A is called up to face a chosen team member from Team B.
- The teacher will pose a question, and the students can either write their answers on the chalk or marker board, be the first to ring a bell, grab an object, or provide a response in a chosen technology platform.
- Points will be awarded to the first student to answer the questions correctly.
- The next designated students will face off for the subsequent questions.
- The team to accrue the most points wins the game. The teacher can decide to award a prize or allow the victory itself to be enough of a reward.
- The time length of game teaming will vary depending on the length of the content to be reviewed.

Take a moment to assess the value of incorporating Games into your classroom.

1 2 3 4 5 6 7 8 9 10

Word Teaming

The foundation of every discipline entails language acquisition. Every teacher should think of powerful and enriching ways to help students learn core vocabulary words. Research shows that developing a sophisticated register will benefit students in their classroom performance and future careers.[4]

How to Facilitate Word Teaming?

- Divide students into several small groups of teams.
- Each team can be given a list of classroom vocabulary words.
- One group member can be assigned the facilitator role of challenging group members to define the vocabulary words. Or, the facilitator role can rotate among team members.
- Group members can take turns defining the words individually or as a team.
- Team members can receive points for answering correctly, or not.
- An added twist can involve teams matching up against each other to see who can define the words first.
- The individual student or team who defines the most words can be recognized and honored, and/or receive points for the activity.

Take a moment to assess the value of incorporating Word Teaming into your classroom.

1 2 3 4 5 6 7 8 9 10

Panel Teaming

Having students assemble together as expert panelist teams can be very effective. Teachers can help students pretend that they are experts about a certain topic, and then they can prepare a panel presentation for their classmates.

How to Facilitate Panel Teaming?

- Students should be divided into various learning teams and given an assigned reading topic.
- One student should be designated as the chairperson of the panel.
- The students should work together to read the material and then break up the information into individual portions.
- Each member will be responsible to summarize the main points of his/her reading section.
- The group will come before the entire class in a panel discussion to present their ideas.
- The chairperson of the team will lead the panel members in sharing out their ideas to the class.

Take a moment to assess the value of incorporating Panel Teaming into your classroom.

1   2   3   4   5   6   7   8   9   10

Debate Teaming

Debate teaming entails students coming together to engage in formal, critical discussions about important issues. Traditionally, the issues discussed are controversial in nature and allow for pros and cons to be considered.

How to Facilitate Debate Teaming?

- Teachers should divide students into small group teams.
- Each team should be provided with the same topic or different ones for discussion. A sample topic for consideration might be: "Women should not be priests" or "Women should be allowed to be priests."
- Allow the teams time to discuss the topic and/or gather information to help them frame their positions.
- Students should be advised that they do not have to necessarily agree with the position that they argue.
- The teams should take turns debating their positions.
- Midway through the debate, ask the teams to switch positions of their argument.
- Following the exercise, debrief with the students and discuss how the activity broadened their understanding.

Take a moment to assess the value of incorporating Debate Teaming into your classroom.

1   2   3   4   5   6   7   8   9   10

Design Thinking Teaming

Design Thinking Teaming is an active engagement approach where students come together to create something challenging and new. The created projects will vary in nature and complexity, but in general they involve creating projects that entail using skills that involve a STEAM (science, technology, engineering, art, and applied mathematics) focus.

According to STEAM Studio cofounders Reid and Sonnenberg, the Design Thinking term was originally conceived by Tim Brown, president and CEO of IDEO, a global product innovation and design firm. The process also has foundational components rooted in the Bloom's Taxonomy framework and incorporates multiple intelligences.[5]

The original process included five components; however, the STEAM Studio cofounders expanded and modified the process and language to include a seven-step design.

How to Facilitate Design Thinking Teaming?

- **Observe**: Students should prepare to ask, listen, empathize, and think about a problem or interest to pursue.
- **Interpret**: Students work together to frame a specific problem.
- **Challenge**: The group identifies and lays out a perspective to pursue and grounds ideas in research.
- **Ideate**: Discussion and pursuit of several ideas are explored.
- **Prototype**: In this phase, students experiment and try out all sorts of ideas as a group.
- **Evolve, Revolve, Focus, Test**: The group begins to refine and test their ideas as a group and solicit feedback from user groups, customers, or peer audiences.
- **Pitch**: This phase is the communication and exhibition phase where groups gather to share their design creations.

Take a moment to assess the value of incorporating Design Thinking Teaming into your classroom.

1   2   3   4   5   6   7   8   9   10

SUPPORTING TEAMS

There are certainly a number of team activities a teacher can implement in the classroom. This chapter describes some of the most practical and easy to implement possibilities.

Regardless of the chosen team activity, the teacher must be the biggest cheerleader in supporting the work of each team and team member learner.

This means the teacher must strongly champion the efforts of every single student participant. The amount of support the teacher provides will vary per student, but the important thing is that the teacher must not neglect any student, regardless of his/her ability level. Connecting and caring about each student's efforts and learning are essential.

This level of teacher connection must hold true every single time students are grouped together for team learning. The teacher's demeanor and enthusiasm is crucial in setting the example in helping to motivate students to care about their team work. Providing support to all learners is a core duty. A teacher can illustrate their support and interest by doing the following:

- The teacher can show care by listening and participating in conversation with each team learner about their specific task at hand.
- The teacher can remind the entire team of learners of the agreed upon norms in advance of every single cooperative learning activity.
- The teacher can conference with team learners about their overarching comprehensive class objectives and explain how their team learning aligns with their learning goals.

MANAGING CHALLENGES OF TEAM LEARNING

Successful use of teaming as a strategy requires patience. Despite the teacher's careful planning in designing effective teams and activities, unexpected challenges may occur. Some team members may not get along well in their groups.

Harnessing the Power of Teaming 107

Figure 3.2 Holly McGee and Harper McGee. *Source:* Photography by Bill McGee.

It is possible that some team members will be too quiet and withdrawn. In referencing some of the worst-case scenario behaviors of team members, Team Manager Kris Bordessa suggests that team members can be bossy, hesitant, grabby, or negative.[6]

A teacher must be prepared to intervene should a team's functioning breakdown. The teacher should not automatically disband the team or team activity the moment a problem emerges, but instead focus on providing some careful interventions.

- Remind the group of the team norms and activity purpose.
- Allow each team member to express their concerns.
- Ensure that each team member is made aware of his/her critical role in the group.
- Be prepared to implement disciplinary classroom management consequences if needed.

Hopefully, these specific interventions will create and restore healthy team functioning. Should there still be problems after these suggestions, perhaps it will make a difference to remove a disruptive team member or two, and/or reconfigure the class group configurations entirely.

The important thing to remember is that using teaming strategies are very effective and well worth the effort to enhance student learning. Creating effective team cultures requires a teacher to stay the course when managing difficulties that may arise.

GRADING TEAMING PROJECTS

There are many ways that team projects can be graded, so it is incumbent upon teachers to determine their own goals, best practices, and rubrics. Students should be informed in advance of any team activity how they will be assessed. In many instances, a teacher may want to structure team projects to cut down on the burden of grading a huge quantity of individual papers.

Specifically, instead of having to grade thirty-five individual research projects, a teacher can cut down on his/her grading load by dividing the class into five groups of seven members, and thereby just have to grade a cumulative total of five team papers! Of course, not every assigned paper should be a team project, but there are times when the strategy can make perfect sense.

For other occasions, a team project may not necessarily entail receiving grades or points. A teacher must help students understand that occasionally they will come together to brainstorm or just to have fun. Furthermore, some group teaming activities may require them to come together over a series of days or weeks, so perhaps the end grade will be given after a team presentation concludes.

Another excellent idea is for students to assess their own performance themselves. This assessment can entail each student evaluating his/her own contribution to the team project using a specific scoring guide system, or the team can grade themselves as a collective unit. The students might rate the quality of their team project aspects on a scale of 1(low) to 10 (high).

In addition, another wise follow-up consideration is for students to reflect on their own learning. Perhaps they can write a final reflection to summarize their understanding.

Many can probably recall unpleasant memories of team projects where some group members do not perform their fair share of the work, or the contribution level is very subpar. This aspect is certainly a legitimate concern, so teachers must devise fair criteria that will not penalize hardworking team members. The teacher must come up with fair, reasonable measures to guard against this problem.

Parents may also raise concerns about the fairness of grades based on team project activities, so teachers must be prepared to justify how individual grades are not impeded because of unprepared team member performance. It is recommended for group team grades to be used in a balanced manner, so that a teacher does have the opportunity to assess individual performance, as well.

This chapter explains why teaming is an excellent teaching strategy to enhance student learning. The teacher plays an important role in establishing clear norms and expectations before students work together in teams. Teachers must structure teams together after careful consideration and thought.

There are a variety of possible team activities such as Research Teaming, Group-Think Teaming, Chart Matrix Teaming, Concentric Circles Teaming, Literature Teaming, Design Thinking Teaming and Game Teaming that will benefit and excite students of all ages. A teacher should not disengage from students when they are working in teams but instead monitor and listen very carefully to each student's contributions.

The teacher will be able to make assessments about each student's understanding based on their participation in the team activities. When and if teams experience conflicts, the teacher must guide the teams back to the established norms and expectations. Teachers can choose to grade team projects or not depending upon the intended learning goals. By harnessing the power of teaming, teachers will be better equipped to meet the learning needs of their students.

NOTES

1. Riley, Dave, San Juan, Robert, Klinker, Joan, and Ramminger, Ann. *Social and Emotional Development: Connecting Science and Practice in Early Childhood Settings* (St. Paul, MN: Redleaf Press, 2008), p. 39.

2. Larmer, John. Boosting the Power of Projects. *Educational Leadership Magazine*, 72 (1), September 2014. p. 42.

3. Kubiszyn, Tom, and Gary D. Borich. *Educational Testing and Measurement: Classroom Application and Practice*. New York: J. Wiley & Sons, 2003.

4. Levine, Harold, Levine, Norman, and Levine, Robert. *Vocabulary for the College Bound Student* (New York, NY: Amsco School Pubns Inc, 2003), p. 1.

5. Reid, David, and Sonnenberg, Mandi. *Unleashing Creative Genius* (Kansas City, Missouri: Gould Evans and Rockhurst University, 2018), p.64, p. 70.

6. Bordessa, Kris. *Team Challenges: 170+ Group Activities to Build Cooperation, Communication, and Creativity* (Chicago, IL: Zephyr Press, 2006), p 265–268.

Epilogue

As this book has shown, teachers have at their disposal multiple ways to spur learning in their classrooms. Implementing thinking skills, use of technologies, and teaming techniques are surefire methods that work.

It is important for teachers to take time in learning how to apply the techniques. Having an open mind and willingness to try these strategies, repeatedly, is tremendously beneficial. Undoubtedly, some students may respond more readily or positively to particular methods, while other students may experience frustration or even failure. The role of the teacher is to continually reassess what strategies will best meet their students' needs.

On any given day, part of a teacher's responsibility is to determine which tools in the toolkit help students learn. The most important thing for teachers to remember is to stay the course and not to give up on themselves or their students.

Some of the thinking skills shared, for example, may work best for one-to-one teaching scenarios, or work best for elementary students. The teaming approaches might work well for some teachers in larger group settings, or perhaps be most ideal at the secondary level. Identifying optimal technologies to use will be determined through careful exploration. The best approaches are determined by careful planning, monitoring, repeated efforts, and evaluation.

The intent of this book is to arm teachers with practical strategies to increase student learning. Teachers and students will make great progress in the classroom because of thinking skills, use of technologies, and thoughtful teaming.

Bibliography

Bordessa, Kris. *Team Challenges: 170+ Group Activities to Build Cooperation, Communication, and Creativity.* Chicago, IL: Zephyr Press, 2006.

Dunston, P.J. A critique of graphic organizer research. *Reading Research and Instruction*, 31 (2), 57–65, 1992.

Finkel, Donald L. *Teaching with Your Mouth Shut.* Portsmouth: Boynton/Cook Publishers, 2000.

Given, Barbara. Theaters of the mind. *Educational Leadership*, 58 (3), 58–71, 2002.

Guskey, T.R. Lessons of mastery learning! *Educational Leadership*, 52–57, 68 (2), 2010.

Hayes, Heather. Bringing lessons to life. *EdTEch*, 2019.

Jennings, Wayne, and Joan Caulfield. *Bridging the Learning/Assessment Gap: Showcase Teaching.* Lanham, MD: ScarecrowEducation, 2005.

Kubiszyn, Tom, and Gary D. Borich. *Educational Testing and Measurement: Classroom Application and Practice.* New York: J. Wiley & Sons, 2003.

Larmer, John. Boosting the power of projects. *Educational Leadership Magazine*, 72 (1), September 2014.

Levine, Harold, Levine, Norman, and Levine, Robert. *Vocabulary for the College Bound Student.* New York, NY: Amsco School Pubns Inc, 2003.

McKibben, Sarah. *Educational Leadership* 76 (5), February 2019.

Reid, D., and Sonnenberg, M. *Unleashing Creative Genius.* Kansas City, MO: Gould Evans and Rockhurst University, 2018.

Riley, Dave, San Juan, Robert, Klinker, Joan, and Ramminger, Ann. *Social and Emotional Development: Connecting Science and Practice in Early Childhood Settings.* St. Paul, MN: Redleaf Press, 2008.

Index

analogues, 10

Bloom's Taxonomy, 3–4
Book Creator, 89

Chart Matrix Teaming, 99
Choice Boards, 18–20
class meetings, 56–58
committees, 12, 42–44
Concentric Circles Teaming, 99–100

Debate Teaming, 104–5
DeBono, Edward, 7–9
Design Thinking Teaming, 105
Dugga, 88

EdPuzzle, 88
Empirical Scientific Method, 2
Entrepreneurship, 67–68
exchanges, 54–55
exhibitions, 66
Explain Everything, 89

Flipgrid, 88

gallery walk, 38–39
Game Teaming, 101–3

Gardner, 5
Google, 78, 84, 86
Google Drive, 86
grading, 108
graphic organizer, 14–22
Group-Think Teaming, 98–99

iMovie, 89
inductive, deductive thinking, 9
intelligences, 5, 15, 25
iPad, 89

Kahoot, 90
Khan Academy, 80
KWHL, 34–36

leadership camp, 50–52
learned expertise, 61–63
learning pyramid, 11–12, 14
learning strategies, 31, 41–42
Literature Teaming, 100, 101

mental imaging, 33–34
Microsoft Teams, 86–87
Movavi, 89

newspapers, 64–65

norms, 95–96, 106
Notability, 89

OneNote, 87
online learning, 81–82
oral history, 68–69

Pages, 89
Panel Teaming, 103, 104
personalization, 46
personal learning plans (PLPs), 44–48, 50
presentations, 66
Pupil-teacher planning, 63–64

reflection, 13, 28, 68, 71, 108
Research Teaming, 97–98
retrospective strategy, 71–72
role play, 52–53

SeeSaw, 90
Six Thinking Hats, 7–9
Socrates, 1
Socrates Seminar, 36–38

Socrative, 90
sparks, 58–59
SQ3R, 39–40
Structured Note Taking, 26, 28–29
student-centered, 41, 81
student-directed, 46, 82, 83
supporting teams, 106

task forces, 42–44
taxonomy of educational objectives, 3, 19
team challenges, 110
team culture, 94–108
teaming, 93–95, 97
team learning, 106
technology, 75–89
Think-Pair-Share, 31–32

videotaping, 69–70

Wikipedia, 78
Word Teaming, 103

YouTube, 78, 80, 88

About the Authors

Joan Caulfield, PhD, is a former teacher, principal, associate superintendent, and professor of education and is a nationally known staff developer and consultant in teaching and learning. She is coauthor of *Inciting Learning: A Guide to Brain-Compatible Learning* and *Bridging the Learning/Assessment Gap-Showcase Teaching* and was cofacilitator of the ASCD Brain-Compatible Network.

About the Authors

Wayne Jennings, PhD, is a former teacher, principal, superintendent, and adjunct professor and has started eight schools during his career in education. He is the author of *School Transformation* and coauthor of *Inciting Learning: A Guide to Brain-Compatible Learning*, as well as *Bridging the Learning/Assessment Gap-Showcase Teaching*. He also was co-facilitator of the ASCD Brain-Compatible Network.

Siabhan May-Washington, EdD, is currently the President of St. Teresa's Academy High School and a National Board Certified teacher. She is a former high-school English teacher, assistant principal, International Baccalaureate Coordinator, and adjunct professor. She presented *Homework Dilemma* research findings at a National Association of Independent Schools Conference and serves on numerous educational advisory boards.

www.ingramcontent.com/pod-product-compliance
Lightning Source LLC
Chambersburg PA
CBHW070739230426
43669CB00014B/2504